# GRAFT

# TOM SKINNER

# GRAFT

## HOW TO SMASH LIFE

BOSH!

HarperCollins*Publishers*

HarperCollins*Publishers*
1 London Bridge Street
London SE1 9GF

www.harpercollins.co.uk

HarperCollins*Publishers*
Macken House, 39/40 Mayor Street Upper
Dublin 1, D01 C9W8, Ireland

First published by HarperCollins*Publishers* 2023

1 3 5 7 9 10 8 6 4 2

A catalogue record of this book is
available from the British Library

ISBN 978-0-00-864399-7

Printed and bound in the UK using 100%
renewable electricity at CPI Group (UK) Ltd

I would like to dedicate this book to my amazing wife Sinéad and my three beautiful children, Henry, Darla and Roma. Without their love and support, none of this would have been possible. Thank you for always being there for me.

# CONTENTS

# WELCOME TO DINO'S, THE GREATEST CAFE ON EARTH

*'It doesn't matter how many steps you have to take, as long as they are in the right direction.'*

IT'S 5.30 ON a crisp March morning and the sun is just rising over the glorious Thames Estuary. The air smells of mud and money. This is my kingdom. It's where I was born and raised and it's where each morning you'll find me, up at sparrow's fart, on the road and hungry for breakfast and a deal.

The drive I take most mornings from Brentwood in Essex is like a trip through my childhood, past Romford Market, Romford Greyhound track and Golf Kingdom. You can tell you're in the centre of the universe because there are more vans than cars on the road and they all proudly display West Ham stickers on their rear doors.

The A12 is one of the main arteries pumping life into London and it's always moving at this time of the morning, so the ride into the fringes of East London is a smooth 20 minutes, taking care to slow down for the speed cameras that seem to multiply overnight.

This is my normal routine. You've probably bought this book because you've seen me on the box, or maybe on social media, but this is me in my natural habit, in the cab of my trusty Transit, which rattles with an assortment of stock loaded in the back. If you want a mattress, a wine cooler, a case of Prosecco or a cut glass chandelier, I can do you a good price. Moisturiser for the missus? None in stock mate, but I can probably find someone who knows where to get some.

Before we know it, we've crossed the River Lea and reached the entrance to New Spitalfields Market, 31 acres of activity where fortunes are made and lost over crates of cauliflowers and punnets of strawberries. But we're not here to deal in fruit and veg, lovely as it all is. We're here to see what's cooking and to strike some deals for the day, and we'll find them at the furthest end of the market, past the loading bays and forklift trucks, in a plain building on the left made of grey breeze blocks. It doesn't look anything special from the outside, and the toilets that take up half the downstairs space are best given a swerve because market traders aren't the most civilised geezers when it comes to khazi etiquette (it's probably all that fibre in their diet from the fruit and veg).

The clue to what we're here for is written in big letters on the side of the building. This is the home of the world-famous Dino's Cafe and we are heading upstairs for breakfast and a business meeting. This, you lovely, lovely people, is the promised land. It's where dreams are made.

As a way of introduction to me and this book, before I get into the nitty gritty, let me explain a little about this place and why it's so special, because to understand me and my life, you have to understand a bit about Dino's.

Firstly, it's a cafe, not a café. It doesn't have one of those funny little flicks over the 'e'. That's important because it tells you that it's not a smashed avocado sort of place. When you visit for the first time you might walk in, look around and wonder what the fuss is about. The Ivy it ain't. To be fair, Ernie, who owns and runs Dino's, hasn't gone over-board on the décor. There aren't fancy light fittings, the tables are Formica, and the central table is one of those ones where the table and chairs are all connected, like you see in prison movies.

There is a big open kitchen at the back, behind a serving counter. There are always at least five staff working and they are always busy. Even when there are only a handful of customers the place is noisy and always buzzing.

You might notice a few unusual things. There are no menus and no prices. Why? As Ernie will tell you, the menu is whatever you want. Fancy spicy Korean noodles with chicken breast and two poached eggs at 6 a.m. on a Monday morning (and I usually do)? No problem. Sunshine curry with round chips? How many portions? Salt beef bagel with a couple of croissants, scrambled eggs with smoked salmon and a bottle of orange Fanta? Coming right up. If Willy Wonka packed in the chocolate game and decided to open a working men's cafe, this is what he'd create. It's better than any Michelin star restaurant.

There are other mysteries too. Why is there a box of worming tablets and flea treatment for dogs on the window-sill? Who is Dino? It doesn't really matter. What does matter is that this is a proper cafe, which in my humble opinion you can usually tell by the ratio of tea to coffee drinkers and whether they use mugs or cups and saucers. Dino's is a mug of tea type of place.

The food is only one half of the story though, because what makes Dino's such a great place is the people you meet in there. You won't find these types anywhere else in the world. As well as the market workers and the fruit and veg sellers, Dino's also attracts some of the shrewdest, sharpest businesspeople and entrepreneurs you'll find anywhere on the planet. Not that you'd know. These aren't geezers in sharp suits driving flash motors. They wear tracksuits and old jeans and drive vans filled with boxes of stuff to sell.

They have end of lines, seconds, liquidated stock, stuff that the big brands can't sell. These are the market traders and the wholesalers who supply the bargain basement retailers. They strike deals with each other, they move gear around and they meet each morning to see what opportunities the day will bring.

And that's where you'll find me, as the sun comes up, often with some of my mates – Collins or Big Lanks – planning what we're doing, seeing what's cooking, complaining about the footie, eating, ribbing each other and doing business. It's like a magical money factory. I never really know what the day will bring when I head there from home, but by the time I leave I've usually arranged some deals, scribbled a few numbers in my little black book and I have a plan of action for the day.

I could choose to stay in bed, have a lie in, watch the telly, but that's not how you get on in life, is it? Success, money, work, it's never come to me, it's never been handed to me. Everything I've ever had, I've had to go out and work for and that's generally the rule in life. If you sit around waiting for things to come to you, they never do. You have to get off your arse, get out there and find opportunities. Different people find them in different places. I find them in Dino's. Wherever they are, I can guarantee you won't find them in bed, watching *This Morning*.

The blokes in Dino's all have the same mindset. They're all there to do a deal, to turn a penny. And the thing about this way of living is that every day is fun. Every day is different, and you never know where you'll end up. I might get a call from someone who's got 300 gift packs of men's toiletries to shift. Or a hotel in Scotland might message me requesting three dozen mattresses. We might even come across a Soviet-era metal locker from Moscow gifted by a Dubai princess (true story) and have to trawl the antique dealers of Essex to find it a home. It's all in a day's work for the modern-day Del Boys at Dino's.

Where do I fit into all this? I assume that if you've bought this book you've either seen me on telly or you follow my social media. You might have seen me on *The Apprentice*. You might even have just seen this on the shelves and thought, 'That's a bit of me, that is.' You might have seen my photo on the cover and thought, 'He looks like a nice bloke, let's see what he has to say.' You might just have thought, 'That book will look nice on my shelves when I'm on a Zoom call.' Well, despite all these different activities, at heart I'm a trader. I'm part of the Dino's family.

So, whatever your reasons for parting with your hard-earned cash and having a read, I'll give you a short potted history of me and how I've ended up in a book in your house.

I'm Tom Skinner. I'm a geezer from Romford, East London. I ain't like one of those blokes from *TOWIE* though. I don't wax my chest and I've never been to Turkey to get my teeth bleached. I like old East End pubs, I also like posh bars and a decent restaurant. I love my family and my mates, and I like a cheeky flutter in the bookies. I like Dubai and Marbella, but I'm equally happy on the Isle of Wight, or in Southend. If you ask my family and friends who I am they'll probably say I'm a chancer, I'm a cheeky chappie, I'm a loveable rogue and hopefully they'll say I'm loyal, I'm generous, I'm a laugh, I'm a grafter and I'm dependable.

I'm a market trader from Romford who can sell just about anything except laughing monkeys (more of that later). I've got a knack for making money, or nicking a quid as we call it round my way. I'm even better at spending it, which probably explains why I've been up and down so many times that I've lost count. The important thing is that I keep trying, and no matter whether I'm at Smith's of Wapping enjoying the finest fillet of Dover Sole or in a Harvester having a burger, you'll usually find me with a smile on my face. My glass is permanently half full (Stella, if you're buying).

I grew up in and around Romford and the East End of London. I'm not academically qualified for anything and I got kicked out of school before I turned 14, so I started grafting instead. A strong work ethic was instilled in me from a young age and I was doing a paper round when I was 12. I loved making money, but I was never your banker or broker type. I'm dyslexic so I struggle with paperwork and forms. I found my passion when I first started working at the weekend on a stall in Romford Market and became one of the regular traders there. I expanded my business and had a few brushes with the law. I set up a company selling pillows and one selling beds. I've tried my hand at lots of things. I've tried investments and stocks and shares, but like a moth to a flame I always end up back where I started, behind a stall in a market, having banter with the punters.

Things changed for me when I went on *The Apprentice* in 2019. I wasn't planning to be a telly personality but my lovely wife Sinéad decided it would be a good idea and filled in the application form for me. At the time I was trying to get my pillow business off the ground, and she decided that a few hundred grand of Alan Sugar's readies would come in handy, as would his advice and business contacts. I laughed when she told me she was sending off the form.

'*The Apprentice* don't have people like me on,' I said. 'I don't work in the City, I don't wear suits, I never went to University.'

Turned out *The Apprentice* did have people like me on. I can only guess I was the novelty act that year.

Things went mental after that.

Then lockdown happened and the other bit of luck that got me to where I am now happened. I was busy delivering mattresses and bedding around the country to all the people who found themselves locked in at home and I started posting videos online while I was out grafting. I'm not a social media influencer, I don't really know what that is to be honest. I see a lot of people on Instagram posting stuff, but none of it makes me feel good about myself or influences me to do something other than swipe to another account. But I like to help people and I like to motivate them because we all need a pick-me-up sometimes, so I started putting messages out there, initially just to let people know where I was working and where they could buy a mattress from, but I always added a little message at the end to try and perk people up, and to let them know that the situation wouldn't last and that they could get through it. 'Hello, you lovely, lovely people. You might be tired, you might be fed up, but it's nearly the end of the week. Keep going, you'll get there and on Friday, there's a lovely cold pint of beer waiting for you as a reward.' That sort of thing. People seemed to like it. I don't know why, but they did. As far as I could tell, I wasn't doing anything special and as I'm not a social media expert I didn't really follow the comments or the number of likes, but mates told me people were taking notice. *That's good*, I thought. *If I can make people happy and brighten a few days up, I'm happy with that.* I didn't plan on it going any further than that. To be fair, I haven't really planned for any of this to happen, but it has and here I am, getting offers to do TV shows, and sitting on panels with politicians discussing the important matters of the day, like why cash-less parking is wrong on every level and why the best indicator of a healthy economy is whether people can afford a pint after work on a Friday afternoon.

It's also why I'm sitting here, typing with one finger trying to write a book that you might enjoy reading and that might even give you a bit of a pick-up.

Now, I'll be honest, I have had a bit of help from people who know about book stuff. Like I said, I've got dyslexia and I can guarantee that if I was left to do this on my own, without a bit of guidance from some experts, you would have got to about page two before you shouted 'none of this makes sense' and headed to the recycle bin. But what I can promise you is that everything you read in the following pages are my words and my thoughts.

I haven't done the usual autobiography-type thing for two reasons: a) my mind doesn't work like that. Have you ever sat down and tried to piece your life together from birth to present day? It's fucking hard work, and while I'm not shy of a bit of graft, it's not my idea of fun; and b) more importantly, I wanted to write something that will be useful. So, while you will find plenty of stories from my life and hopefully, you'll learn some things about me that you wouldn't have known (and that hopefully won't get me arrested), you'll also get some helpful stuff too, and stuff that might motivate you to go out there and smash it, even if you're going through tough times or struggling, because we all do. It's important to remember that you can't win all the time, and it doesn't matter how many times you get knocked down, what's important is the number of times you get back up.

## CHAPTER 1

# THERE'S SOMETHING IN THE WATER IN THESE PARTS

*'Don't go home until you are proud of what you've done today.'*

WHO DOESN'T LOVE a bit of dinner, right? It was fate that I walked into Dino's one December morning on the way to making some furniture deliveries. A mate had a wholesale furniture place around the corner and I'd gone over to pick up some stock. He told me about a cafe he went to in Smithfield Market, and as I was driving to Wales that day he suggested I fill up with a proper breakfast before I headed off.

I like to think I'm a bit of a cafe connoisseur and when I first walked in I could tell there was something special about the place. It was full of geezers hunkered down over plates piled high with proper food. There wasn't a chai seed in sight. *Fuck me*, I thought, *some of these blokes are eating curry*. It was, to coin another common phrase from my neck of the woods, a bit of me. And then I saw that they were serving Christmas dinner and I was hooked. It was love at first sight. It was 5 a.m., we had a long trip ahead of us and a plate of turkey with all the trimmings seemed like a good way to fuel up before setting off, so I ordered one.

There was a lot of debate in the cafe that year because Ernie the owner was adamant that Yorkshire puddings had no place at the Christmas dinner table. The punters were split 50/50 over whether he should start serving them. He stuck by his guns. Yorkshires were banned. Who knows who's right or wrong. It's an argument as pointless as whether you put jam or cream first on a scone, or whether you say scone as in stone, or scone as in gone. And is it milk first then tea, or tea then milk? I've never actually asked Ernie for his opinions on these matters of national importance.

Anyway, after that first Christmas dinner I went back for the next 21 days running and had the same order each time. I probably would have carried on after Christmas, but Ernie took the crowd pleaser off the menu.

We were doing a lot of long-distance deliveries all over the UK that year, from Devon to Newcastle and Scotland. The firm was fuelled by Dino's breakfasts. They were addictive, like a calorie-loaded version of crystal meth.

At that stage in my life I'd done *The Apprentice*, and one day Ernie came over to me and said, 'You look like that bloke off *The Apprentice*.'

'I *am* that bloke off *The Apprentice*,' I told him.

There's something special about the place and it gets me going in the morning, not just because of the grub, but the people in there. It's the atmosphere, the 'ambiance' they call it in posh places. Dino's punters are the sort of people you find in any proper old-style cafe in the East End. People are there to have a deal, not just a meal. These places are centres of trade, like some of the old pubs in the East End and Essex too. I've done some of my best deals in cafes and pubs over bacon sarnies or pints of Stella. They are places where like-minded people meet to have a natter and make some money, people who are up for a deal.

Conversations always circle back to the regular subjects: football, who did what last night and who's got what to sell.

'I've got a lorry load of face masks, you interested?'

'I'll have 'em.'

Common exchanges like this happen all the time. You'll always find someone to buy something in a working man's cafe because there's always a market trader, a dealer, an eBayer, an online seller or an auctioneer looking to buy or sell. If you look for it, you'll find it. These are the early birds, the grafters who are out before the office workers are even awake. That's why I love getting up at the crack of dawn and getting out there to smash it. I love buying stock to sell. I'm addicted to it.

You might wonder why I'm banging on about cafes and the people in them, but there's a lesson to be learned from all this and it ain't the secret recipe for Ernie's spicy Korean noodles (he'd never give that away). It's that you become your environment. If you sit at home on your computer all day, you miss opportunities and you miss out on life. If you surround yourself with people who are driven and motivated and want to do well, you can't help but get involved in it yourself. It's a cliché but it's true: you make your own luck in life and you don't get lucky if you don't get out there and get among it.

Dino's has become my lucky charm. It's where the videos first started to really take off. One day I sat down in there and decided to film a short video to get people going and give them a little pep talk, so I ordered a steak pie and one of my mates filmed me. I didn't plan anything, it was off the cuff. I just told anyone who was watching to go out there and give it 110 per cent and that if they did, they would succeed. It seemed to hit a nerve because lots of people commented. In that first Dino's video I never mentioned the pie or the cafe, much to Ernie's dismay. The videos became a habit. Each morning I'd sit with my mates in the cafe before work, someone would film me and I'd talk about the day, what I was doing and I'd sign off with a motivational message. They are now watched by people all over the world. One morning my little boy was up all night, so I was knackered and had a day off. At 7.30 in the morning Ernie called me and said, 'Mate, I think you'd better come to the cafe. There's a geezer here from Melbourne, Australia who's come because he's seen the videos.' I went down to meet him. He was a lovely bloke. He told me that he and his mates were fans.

Dino's is one of my favourite places and in a way helped make me who I am, but before that the place which moulded me the most was Romford, where I grew up. If you don't know Romford, let me try and describe it for you. It's like an upmarket Dagenham; like a polished turd (which is not a phrase the estate agents use). If you don't know either Dagenham or Romford, imagine typical towns with high streets and offices and a few parks and you'll get the idea. Dagenham is a few miles outside of the East End and London's Docklands if you head east towards Essex. It's built up and run down. Romford is more your commuter town, not as green and leafy as those boroughs and counties further outside of London but it's broken away from the big city's orbit and has a bit more of a suburban feel to it. It calls itself an historic market town and the market played a big role in the town's life when I was growing up there. Everyone seemed to have something to do with it, whether they were stall holders, customers or people selling stuff to the stall holders. It was a town of commerce.

The first house I lived in was at 30 Sims Close, which was just round the corner from the market. It was a townhouse, it had three floors and two rooms on each floor. It backed onto a park where there was a miniature railway which took children on train rides. There were all these little ride-on engines chugging around the track, maintained by blokes who had outgrown their train sets and moved onto something bigger, like a gateway between toy trains and proper trains. Come to think of it, maybe that's why I was named Thomas.

Our house was also a few hundred yards from Main Road, which as the name suggests was the main route to Romford town centre in one direction and the route out to the flashier parts of Essex the other way, like Brentwood, where I live now. To me, it felt like Main Road was paved with gold when I was a kid. It wasn't, it was lined with a Harvester and shops, but I always felt that when I hooked a right onto it and pedalled my bike towards places like Gidea Park and Gallows Corner, opportunity awaited. Mainly because most of my mates lived that way.

I lived with my mum, who worked in a call centre and helped people when their boilers broke down, and my dad, who worked the markets and always had a business opportunity on the go. I lived there with my brother and sister and it was an idyllic, normal upbringing.

I've got great memories of growing up and being a kid. Romford used to be the best gaff in the world. When I was a kid, the market was always mobbed and I went there every Saturday morning on my bike, which I had to get off and push around because there were so many people. Everyone who worked the stalls was having it, nicking a few quid. The air was filled with shouts, the sounds of cash changing hands and the smell of fried food. It was heaven.

I had loads of friends and was given lots of freedom because both my parents grafted. My mates remember me back then as the type of kid who would always be out getting involved in mischief. I was chatting to one friend the other day who knew me when I was nine and she said, 'Tom, no one ever knew where you came from, you were this little kid who turned up randomly from nowhere.' I was a latchkey kid. Sometimes I'd get into trouble, I was naughty but not what I'd call 'bad' naughty. I was a bit of a cheeky chappie. I knocked a mate's wall down once by accident when I crashed my mini-motorcycle into it. I was about 12. That was the stupid kind of stuff I got myself involved in.

I always wore a white vest or t-shirt, a pair of Timberland boots and a pair of jeans, in all weathers. That was my uniform, and I was still rocking the same style into my late teens before I started to earn a bit and could afford to expand my wardrobe with some of the knocked-off designer gear that everyone seemed to be able to get hold of in the area in those days.

One thing I always did was graft. I always had a job because it was instilled in me from my parents that if I wanted anything other than the basic food and board they were obliged to provide as my guardians, and if I wanted anything beyond George at Asda in my wardrobe, I'd have to get it myself with my own money, which I was expected to earn. This did not seem unreasonable to me, and it was very common for my peers to be out working too. I think the rules around children working were a bit less strict then. We weren't chimney sweeps or child labour, it was more your normal Saturday jobs and paper rounds, both of which

I had. I got up early every morning in all weathers to shove copies of the *Sun*, the *Star* and the *Mirror* through letterboxes in Romford. Thankfully there weren't so many *Times* and *Telegraph* readers in the area, so the weekend round wasn't as heavy as it could have been. I found ways to earn extra too. Me and a mate, Ollie, had a nice little sideline going, washing cars for a fiver. We lugged a bucket and sponge around and knocked on doors. We weren't great at it, mainly we just smudged the dirt around, but most of our customers took pity and paid us anyway. We went carol singing for pound coins at Christmas and did penny-for-the-Guy before Fireworks Night. We were always looking for ways to make money.

I don't want to sound like an old fart, but they were more honest days. Nowadays kids go out and nick bikes and phones. Back then we knew that if we wanted money, we had to work for it. No one would think about nicking another kid's bike, you didn't stitch up your neighbours, you looked out for each other. Then again, you didn't have £5,000 carbon fibre frames and all that silliness back then. My bike was a Kona. It was worth a couple of hundred new, max. Second hand, it wasn't worth nicking.

Entertainment as a kid revolved around watching West Ham play football (which also taught you to cope with heartache and disappointment), building ramps in the park to ride your bike over and going to the cinema. We had a paintball gun too, which we often took over to the park and chased each other around with. When I was older, we also got a child's quad bike which I used to ride around on.

We had global cuisine on the doorstep. For Chinese food there was the Ming Court, which shut and reopened as the Wa Ping, and the Blue Orchid, and for Indian food we had the Café Raj and Zaafran which were to die for. I still eat at Zaafran today.

Dad used to drink in a pub called The Ship, next door to Ming Court, and I used to go in and see him after school and have a chat with him and his mates if they were there.

We had family holidays when I was little but not loads because my parents were always working. We were left to get on with it and make our own entertainment in the holidays, although Christmas was always the bollocks because there were a lot of us (I have loads of cousins) and that was when all the extended family got together.

My big thing when I was young was sports. I used to play tennis at the Gidea Park Tennis Club. I played football in the park, I did some boxing and was good at rugby. I was lucky enough never to break any bones. My favourite sport was golf. My dad's dad, granddad Harry Skinner, got me into it. He was a really keen golfer and used to play every weekend. He got me my first clubs and I loved hitting balls and got some lessons when I was 10 or 11. It was an unusual pastime for a kid from Romford to get involved in back then, but one of my mates also used to play at the same golf club so I had someone else my age to share a round with. I still have the same gloves I had when I was 15.

Harry Skinner was the guvnor and he died when I was 12. It's a shame I didn't get to know him more, because by all accounts he was a legend in Essex and the East End. Everyone knew him. One day when I was much older I was in one of my locals, The New Inn in Romford (another environment that moulded me and which I'll talk about later) and on this particular day I was in the pub with my mates having a laugh when an old bloke sitting on a stool nursing a pint, who must have been in his eighties, grabbed my arm.

He looked me in the eye, pointed at my face and said, 'You're a Skinner, ain't you son?'

'Yeah, I am,' I frowned.

'I fucking knew it, all you Skinners are the same,' he chuckled. 'Larger than life and loud.'

'What you talking about mate?' I asked.

'Your granddad was a legend in these parts, son. I knew him, and years ago he saved me from a right hiding.'

The geezer then proceeded to tell me his story.

After the war, he did national service at a camp in the area. My granddad was there the same time, and they became friends. Funny enough, it was the same place that the famous gangsters Ronnie and Reggie Kray did their national service.

'I was about 17,' the bloke told me. 'Your granddad was older and he was a big, strong man. I wasn't and he took me

22

under his wing and looked after me. All the blokes in charge were horrible bullies. They regularly came into the barracks unannounced to do inspections. You had to stand there with your boots in your hands to show them how shiny they were. Your granddad always got someone else to do his boots for him and they were always squeaky clean.

'One day this sergeant burst in and told everyone to stand by their bunks with their boots. He was a particularly nasty bastard. I hadn't cleaned my boots that morning so I knew I was going to get punished. We lined up in front of our beds and the bloke barked: "Harry, show us your boots!" Harry's boots were shiny and he passed the test. The sergeant then asked to see mine. They were filthy.'

The bloke told me that he was about to get a whack from the sergeant when my granddad stepped in front of him.

'He told that bully, "leave him alone or I'll land one on you."' The old man chuckled at the memory. 'The sergeant shit himself and backed off and Harry saved me from getting a hiding. I always remembered that but we lost touch after we got out.'

Then he looked at me and said, 'You're the double of your granddad. You look like him, you walk like him, you talk like him. Everything about you, it's him.'

I was touched by that and the following week the old man came in with a photo of him and my granddad together in their uniforms. He was right, I looked just like my granddad.

Family has always been important to me, and both my mum and dad have been big influences on me. Later in my teens they split up, and that did affect me because I loved family life. It was a period of instability and no one likes going through things like that. But I'm also of the opinion that if you are in an unhappy relationship and you've tried to work things out, it's best to call it a day, especially if it threatens to upset other people around you.

When you're a kid and your parents split up, you think the world is going to end. It's something that lots of families go through nowadays, and for the kids it is a time of insecurity and disruption. Parents always need to consider their kids in these situations. Don't use them as punch bags or as a way of getting back at each other. The most important thing for a kid is that they feel loved and they have some form of stability. It's hard for everyone, but if you are sensible and behave like grown-ups there's no reason why your children won't adapt and cope at the end of it. Time is a great healer and eventually things work themselves out.

After they split, I had periods where I lived with my mum and my dad and I'm close to both. My mum is the loveliest person in the world. She is caring and kind and she's tough. She has always been there, she's the homely type who cooks for everyone and looks after everyone, whereas my dad is a bit more of a livewire and a geezer and likes to go to the pub and have a beer. He is a legend. He's a ducker and diver and a grafter like me. We are very similar.

They both taught me that in life you have to learn to turn the hard times into good times. Learn from your challenges. Life is never going to be a bed of roses all the time. Accept that there will be tough times, and in those tough times get your head down and push through. There's no point sitting around feeling sorry for yourself. Sometimes life is hard, but you can deal with it and remember, tough times don't last, tough people do.

Things got more stable and as a family we worked out new ways moving forward. Dad remarried and I got two step-brothers and a step-sister. They've all got proper jobs.

So that was my childhood, in a nutshell. I grew up in a place that was full of characters and people on the make, who worked hard and played hard and knew the value of graft. If there was one big lesson I learned, it was that life doesn't owe you a living. If you want to make something of yourself, you have to make it happen for yourself. You have to get on with it and get your head down. And when you do, if you give it 110 per cent, you will succeed.

Now I've done alright for myself, I've moved to Brentwood which is like the Beverly Hills of Essex. It's best known as the place where they filmed *The Only Way Is Essex*. Anyone from Romford who does well for themselves moves to Brentwood. For the Skinner family it's like a natural progression out from Romford in the East End over the generations and then into Brentwood. In America in the old days people used to move west to find their fortunes; in my gaff they move east. The main similarity is that in doing so, we all became cowboys.

In Brentwood we have proper posh places like bakeries that do San Francisco sourdough and serve fancy coffee in cups without handles. I don't know what Ernie would make of it.

It hasn't always been like that. Back in the nineties, pre-Sugar Hut days (the bar where the *TOWIE* mob used to meet and bitch about each other), Brentwood was known as a boring place where people went to retire. Then *TOWIE* happened and property prices shot up. One of my dad's mates from Stratford way bought a house on one of the new housing developments in Brentwood and paid £250,000 for it about ten years ago when the place was a nothing town. Now his gaff is worth £1.8 million. No one was bothered about the town until TV put it on the map. There was even a *TOWIE* bus tour like you get in Beverly Hills to see the famous locations and the homes of the celebs. One of the stops on the route was a big mental asylum which had been developed into an exclusive housing estate with apartments where some of the *TOWIE* people lived. Several of the *TOWIE* gang cashed in by opening shops on the high street. We had beauty salons and fashion boutiques. The older residents quite liked it because it brought a lot of money and kudos to the town and pushed their house prices up.

Brentwood residents tend to be just as entrepreneurial as the people from Romford and Dagenham, they just have more money to throw around. It's like most of the people in this region have an ability to recognise an opportunity when it arises and we're not afraid of hard work. There's something in the water here, a mentality shared by East Londoners and Essex geezers. Everyone is born to make money. There's this old argument about whether you are born with the skills you display in life or whether you learn them as you go along. They call it nature over nurture. I don't know whether it was destiny that me and the people I grew up with were going to make money, that the ability to nick a quid was always in our genes. Were we naturally adapted to duck and dive, do a deal and graft? I don't know. I think the environment is more important. I learned from the people around me, and what I saw and experienced as I was growing up. Maybe it's because we are between London Docklands and Tilbury Docks, two areas where there's always been a lot of trade and a bit of skulduggery. Who knows? Whatever the answers are, it's a special environment where everyone wants to do well, and everyone's a little bit dodgy.

# SKINNER'S SCRIPTURES

- If you want a Christmas dinner at 5 a.m. then have a Christmas dinner at 5 a.m.

- Find the right environment to help you achieve your goals.

- Get used to hard work, the world doesn't owe you anything.

- Shit happens, but bad times don't last.

- Clean your shoes.

## CHAPTER 2

# LESSONS FROM THE SCHOOL OF HARD KNOCKS

*'Let the monkey conquer the tree and the shark conquer the sea.'*

LIFE IS ALL about learning the right lessons and it's fair to say that school didn't teach me the type of lessons I needed for the life I was born into. Don't get me wrong, I enjoyed it, I had a laugh and I had plenty of friends, but in terms of the learning, let's just say it wasn't my thing.

I worked out later, after I left, that school doesn't teach the important lessons for people like me. What good is knowing how rain clouds are formed, or when the Battle of Hastings was, when you're negotiating the price of a lorry load of mattresses? Since I left school, I've never had to work out the circumference of a circle and I've never been asked to dissect a frog. I'm not sure that anyone does that in their normal working lives. It's got to be one of the most pointless things that you ever do at school. All those poor frogs killed in the name of science just for the sake of maybe one or two people in the country each year who go on to live the dream and become frog scientists.

Reading and writing and general arithmetic come in useful, but where school failed me and millions of other kids who leave and set up businesses is in the life skills department. School doesn't teach those general skills that are really important. No one at my school taught me to open a bank account, no one taught me about paying rent or saving money or budgeting. No one taught me the basics of how to deal with everyday life. So I left school knowing how to write my name, do fractions and open an email, but no one taught me whether this handbag was better than that handbag, or what to do when people are trying to get one over on you. More life skills are needed. I didn't fail at school but I wasn't interested.

I didn't do so well for two main reasons. Firstly, I looked at the adults in my life and realised that what I was being taught was not really going to be relevant for the type of life I was going to be living. I had ambitions. I wanted to be a businessman and buy and sell. I wanted to work for myself. Nothing on the curriculum was geared towards helping me achieve that goal. Secondly, I am dyslexic. I am intelligent but I struggled with certain tasks. When I read things, I miss words. For example, the sentence might be 'the cat walked down the road' and I see 'the cat down road'. As a result, nothing made sense when I was reading things at school. And my brain thinks quicker than I can write, so when I write, I skip words. To this day, I can't fill out a form. There's a mental block whenever I'm presented with one, be it a parking ticket or the online form for the Dart charge which you have to pay when you go over the Dartford

Crossing. I just can't seem to do it. I'm lucky that throughout my life I've had people around me who have helped out when I've needed it.

My dyslexia was recognised at school which meant I was given ten minutes more in my exams so I could ask the invigilator for guidance if I didn't understand the question, but I was a blagger so I just blagged the answers anyway. I made up for my lack of academic success by always being someone's mate, always getting on with people, and I realised that if you get on with people, they will always help you. I was a popular kid at school, the teachers liked me, but I was always the cheeky one. I was naughty, but not 'naughty' naughty, if you know what I mean. I was a joker and a chancer, not a troublemaker.

By the time I did my GCSEs, my heart wasn't in it. I'd been chucked out of school by that stage anyway. In my defence, I believe it was a minor offence and that if you looked at it objectively, I was actually showing a great deal of entrepreneurial promise. The school looked at it rather differently.

I showed early business acumen at secondary school by asking my mum to buy bulk loads of cakes or sweets cheaply that I then sold at a profit to my classmates, thereby mastering the theory of wholesale and retail while my peers were struggling with long multiplication. Everyone was happy. They got sweets and chocolate cheaper than the school canteen, while I made a small mark-up per item.

I enjoyed making money, which is why I worked from a young age, firstly doing a paper round and then when I was a bit older I got a Saturday job in a barber's shop. The shop was run by a mate of my dad's. He'd been in prison and when he was inside, he learned to cut hair. When he came out and went on the straight-and-narrow he opened a barber shop up in Romford and Dad put in a good word for me. As a result, each Saturday morning after my paper round I had my Shreddies and then headed off to the town on my bike where I spent the day sweeping hair off the floor and hanging out with a former armed robber. He was a lovely bloke and very handy with the clippers.

Anyway, the point is I liked working and was always open to new opportunities. I liked to spend money too. There was a bagel shop in the high street that everyone used to go to, but the bagels were £3 which was quite expensive back then, especially for a kid. I was a regular though, because with my jobs and the school enterprise I was on around £60 a week aged 14, so I was the bagel king. I think that's where I got my taste for the finer things in life.

As I got older, I found more ways to make money. I set up market stalls for the traders at the weekend as well. I earned more and as I was living with my dad at the time, he told me I had to pay rent. Dad made me pay rent when I was a kid. At the time I thought he was taking liberties, but I understand now. He wanted to teach me a lesson and would always end up giving it back to me when I was short. In fact, I often went to him when I needed a few quid for something and he'd usually bung me a fiver or a tenner and say, 'Mate, if you want money you need to go and earn it.' One day we were having the usual discussion we had when I needed a few extra quid for something or other and he said, 'I might be able to set you up with something to help. Give me a couple of days and I'll let you know.'

A few days later I got home from rugby training covered in mud and Dad and his mate Alan – we called him Uncle Alan not because he was related, but because he looked like Uncle Albert from *Only Fools and Horses* – were in the lounge. They'd been to the pub and they had a suitcase on the floor.

'This is for you,' Dad said, handing it to me.

It was heavy. I opened it up, looked inside and my eyes widened. It was full of DVDs in their little plastic covers. At first glance some of them looked like movies I recognised. Then I looked more closely.

*Forrest Hump*. Then another. *Schindler's Fist*.

The penny dropped. They were porn movies.

Dad and Alan were laughing as I leafed through them.

'It's a way for you to make a few quid. Knock 'em out at £3 each or two for a fiver and give me back a pound for each one you sell. All your mates are going to want them,' Dad said.

Of course, I knew he was right. At school I had a target market of literally hundreds of teenage boys.

'Sweet,' I grinned. I could see a very profitable endeavour taking shape.

The next day I went to school, whacked the suitcase in my locker and stuffed a handful of 'stock' in the little drawstring JD Sports bag I carried around with me. Then I started knocking them out. It still ranks as one of the best lines of stock I've ever shifted. I probably could have charged double. You have to remember that was in the mid-noughties before free porn sites and before most people had broadband or Wi-Fi or smartphones. DVDs and mags were still the only way teenagers could access a bit of smut. Consequently, as far as the male pupils were concerned, I was the most popular kid in school. Word spread quickly. Teenage boys and porn are made for each other, and I made about £200 on my first day.

*This is easy, much better than cheap chocolate bars*, I thought.

I was flush with cash every day and in the canteen I was the boss, throwing cash around like it was going out of fashion.

'I'll have the sausage casserole, a side of chips, jam roly-poly and double custard please. Throw in a Penguin and a Ribena as well.'

And it was in the canteen during one of these spending sprees that it all unravelled. As I leaned over to get a carton of juice from the chiller, my trusty JD Sports bag split. It had been overstuffed with stock for the lunchtime trade. My merch spilled out all over the floor of the lunch hall.

One of the teachers who didn't like me saw what happened and walked over as I was stooping down to pick them up.

'What are these?' he asked as he bent down and picked one up to inspect it.

He turned over a copy of *Shaving Ryan's Privates* in his hand and his eyes nearly popped out of his head.

'Come on sir, you know what they are, they're porno DVDs obviously,' I shrugged.

His face went red. I couldn't tell if he was angry or embarrassed. He ordered me to go straight to his office while he bent down and collected the evidence.

*Here we go*, I thought. *This isn't going to end well.*

I sat in his office on my own, contemplating my fate for ten minutes before he came in. He didn't have my DVDs.

'Where are they sir? Can I have them back, I haven't paid for them yet,' I asked.

He couldn't believe what he was hearing.

'Of course, you can't. They've been confiscated and sent to the headmaster, which is where I am taking you,' he said.

I was marched to the head's office and sat outside while the head and the teacher worked out what to do with me, I assume.

Eventually, the first teacher came out and told me to go in. By then my locker had been opened and the suitcase had been found. I knew this because when I walked into the head's office there were loads of DVDs on his desk.

'You do know it's wrong to sell these?' he asked, gesturing to the pile on his desk.

'I know sir, I just wanted to make a few quid. I wanted some new trainers and a new Lacoste tracksuit,' I explained.

'I'm going to have to ring your parents,' the head told me.

I hoped he'd ring my mum because she was more level-headed. She would have apologised and said I was a naughty boy and assured him it wouldn't happen again. But the head rang my dad, who came to the school about half an hour later.

The three of us sat in the stuffy office and to his credit Dad started to try and get me off the hook and explain things in his own way.

'You see, I don't want him growing up to be a spoilt kid,' he said. 'He's got his paper round and his Saturday job, but he wanted a few more quid off me so I saw a fella in the pub, bought the case off him because he looked like he was skint and needed the money and I gave them to Tom to teach him the basics of how to buy and sell.'

The head looked stunned. I don't think he could get his head round the fact that Dad was trying to justify that me selling porn to my classmates was actually a good thing.

'You do know they're illegal?' the head asked. 'Your son is selling illegal and obscene contraband to the pupils. I can't have that in my school. I'll have to call the police.'

'Come on now,' said Dad, 'That's not necessary. I'll take the blame, and I can assure you it won't happen again.'

Things didn't work out well. The discussion got a bit more heated. Dad called him a 'helmet' and we left. That was my last day at school. I was 14 but they let me go back two years later to do the exams. By the time I did, I'd already started working on the markets. I was done with education. I never went to college or university; I jumped into the world of work at the deep end.

A lot of young people get anxious and stressed about their exams. I did too and worried that without exams I wouldn't amount to anything because that's what I'd been led to believe. Now I tell kids not to stress themselves out too much. If you don't get the results you hoped for, it's not going to change your life. That doesn't mean you should give up, but I've sat in boardrooms with the biggest businesspeople in the UK and I've never once been asked how many GCSEs I've got, or whether I did a degree. Work hard, do your best but don't get stressed because you'll be fine if you don't get the grades you want.

A lot of people leave school feeling like they've failed, and they shouldn't. Just because you don't pass exams doesn't make you a failure. Far from it. It just means you haven't found what you are good at.

Everyone has a skill. Everyone can do something. My skill is talking to people and selling. I'm not really a good businessperson, but I'm a good money-making person. I can make a quid and if you put me in a room with anyone, no matter who they are, I will talk to them and get on with them. That's my skill.

My advice to anyone struggling to get on is to find what you are good at and focus on that. Build on it. Strengthen your strengths, don't try to strengthen your weaknesses. Monkeys are good at climbing trees, right? Sharks aren't. If a shark decides it wants to be as good as the monkey at climbing trees, it isn't going to end well. *Hang on a minute,* the shark will say to itself, *I've got fins. I'm not built to climb a tree but I'm a fucking good swimmer. I can swim ten times better than the monkey, so I should concentrate on swimming. Let the monkey conquer the tree and I'll conquer the sea.*

We learn throughout life. You should never stop learning. Be like a sponge, absorb everything. When that dry sponge goes in that water it picks up everything, all the water, all the dirt, all the soap. It's all combined in the one sponge and when you squeeze it all out, you release it all somewhere else. My philosophy is to be like that sponge. Meet people, be kind to people, get on with people, be polite and learn from them. Take every opportunity to learn from something, good and bad. I'm a West Ham fan, for example, and anyone who follows the team knows that being an Iron (as West Ham fans are called) involves a lifetime of missed chances and regrets (their 2023 European trophy aside). But even in that there are lessons to be learned. West Ham has taught me how to be resilient and how to be loyal but to not always expect a reward for that loyalty.

Life is full of teachers. Dad has always tried to be one of mine. His lessons have been invaluable and that's another one of the important lessons in life: choose your teachers well. For the kind of life I was destined to have, the teachers at school didn't really turn out to be good teachers for me.

Dad has always tried to look out for me and guide me into making the right decisions. After I was on *The Apprentice*, my bed business did well and I made a decent amount of money. In fact, never in my life had I accumulated that amount of cash, so I did what any clever young entrepreneur would do. I bought myself a silly, big, gold Rolex watch and started looking for a Bentley to buy.

Bentleys were my favourite car in the world. I had always loved them and wanted one. To me, a Bentley was the mark of success. If you owned a Bentley, you'd made it. So, I went on AutoTrader and searched up and down the country for the right make and model. Eventually I found a beautiful black Bentley Continental GT with a golden leather interior. I looked at the photos and it was the car of my dreams. It was for sale in a dealership in Tunbridge Wells in Kent.

I rang Dad.

'I've found one,' I said. 'I've got the money, I'm going to have a look at it.'

'That's fantastic son, I'm so proud of you. I'll come with you,' he replied.

I arranged a time to view the car at the dealership, counted the cash out and threw it in a Tesco carrier bag. Dad came to pick me up. I threw the bag in the back of his car and off we went.

On the way Dad dispensed one of his lessons.

'Look mate,' he started, 'I'm a lot more experienced than you. I've bought and sold thousands of cars and I'm telling you, you've got to be careful of car dealers because obviously they're just trying to lick you over and steal a few quid. There are thousands of motors out there you can buy. What I'm saying is, don't get yourself all excited because we are not going in there and buying the first thing we see.'

*Wise words*, I thought.

He continued. 'I'll look round it and tell you what's wrong with it. It'll be valeted and cleaned and it'll look immaculate but always remember that there may be another better one somewhere else, so don't rush into anything. We ain't gotta buy it today, even if you have got a bag of readies in the back.'

'Alright Dad, I understand what you're saying,' I agreed. 'You're 100 per cent correct.'

No matter what he said about being cautious, I couldn't help being excited. I mean, this was the motor I'd always seen myself driving. I could visualise myself in it, rolling down Main Road, turning heads.

We pulled up to the showroom and just as Dad had predicted, the car was absolutely stunning. It was everything a Bentley should be. The paintwork gleamed in the sunlight. There wasn't a scratch on it. I opened the door and could smell the leather and wood. It had massive 22-inch wheels, and a six-litre W12 engine.

The salesman could see my eyes light up as he handed me the keys.

'Start her up,' he said.

I did and grinned at the deep, throaty roar of the Bentley engine. I was falling in love. I had been weakened, and I knew it. I was enchanted by the car so I looked at Dad, who I had decided was going to be my voice of reason. He too had been looking over the car thoroughly, checking every angle, rubbing his chin, stooping down to look under it. I assumed he was casting an expert, objective eye over it and was going to play the long game with the salesman.

'Well, what do you think?' the salesman asked.

I didn't want to say anything, so I looked at Dad and waited for him to break the spell and say something to burst the bubble. I was relying on him to be the voice of caution. I could see he was thinking it over.

Then he spoke.

'Mate!' he said, throwing his arms in the air. 'This thing is beautiful. Look at it. It's in great nick for the year. I'd have it myself if I had the cash. Tom, you've gotta buy it. You'd be a mug to pass this up.'

He looked at me.

'We'll have it,' he declared.

He was like a kid in a sweet shop. I'd never seen him so animated and excited. I couldn't believe what I was seeing and stood there staring at him, shaking my head. *All that bollocks about don't buy the first one you see, he's worse than me*, I thought.

With Dad as enthusiastic as me, the deal was sealed and within ten minutes I'd been to Dad's car, got my bag of money and plonked it on the desk in the sales office. The salesman, who was expecting me to pay on a card or on finance, didn't know what to do with it.

That was it, I had my first Bentley. I went back a couple of days later to pick it up, after the car had been waxed and prepared. I even bought myself a new coat, new boots and new pair of jeans to wear when I collected it. I loved it. I had nowhere to go but I filled it up with petrol and drove. I shortly realised how expensive Bentleys are to run. It did seven miles to the gallon.

About ten months later, I had to sell it because I needed the money to invest in my company. But those are the ups and downs of life. It was lovely while it lasted.

While Dad's 'buyer beware' lesson fell flat, another one he taught me earlier in life did have an impact.

I was about 18 and staying at Dad's house with my girl-friend at the time. We were in the bedroom upstairs watching the horror film, *Scream*. It was quite late, and I heard Dad come in from the pub. He'd had a few beers and banged on the door, shouted goodnight and went to bed.

About 15 minutes later, my girlfriend grabbed the remote and turned the sound down.

'I can hear someone outside,' she said.

I laughed.

'You're watching a scary film, you're hearing things,' I said. But she was certain she could hear something outside, so I opened the curtains to have a look and to reassure her that it was just her imagination.

'See,' I said, gesturing out the window without turning round. When I did turn and look properly, I saw a dark shape at the front of the house by the door that led to a side building where Dad had a quad bike, a couple of mountain bikes and a lawnmower.

When my eyes adjusted to the shadows, I saw a big bloke with a screwdriver who was trying to force the door open.

'Fuck! Someone's trying to get in!' I shouted and bolted out the room and ran across the landing, banging on Dad's door as I passed it.

'Get up, there's a geezer trying to break in downstairs. Come on!' I shouted.

I was wearing a pair of shorts and a vest. At the time I was working on the markets, and I was probably in the best shape of my life. I was playing rugby at a high level. I was training four times a week. I was boxing and swimming. I was slim and fit. The bloke I'd seen looked big, but I was ready to defend our home.

I ran down the stairs, flew out the front door and the geezer jumped, turned around and tried to stab me with the screwdriver. Instinctively I ducked and hit him square on the chin. He staggered back, then regained his balance and went for me again. Something clicked inside of me. He was armed with a weapon. I knew I had to stop him and hit him again and knock him down. I continued hitting him. He dropped the screwdriver, but I wasn't prepared to find out if he had a knife or a gun. I couldn't give him the opportunity to pull out another weapon, so I carried on hitting him.

Out of the corner of my eye, I was aware that Dad had come running out the front door behind me. He had a golf club in his hand. As he ran towards me and the intruder he lifted the 9-iron over his head and swung it at me and the bloke on the floor, missed both of us, spun round and went down with a thud into the bushes where he crawled around while I carried on hitting the burglar until I was sure he wasn't going to attack me. I stopped, kicked the screwdriver away and looked down at his face, which was a bloody mess.

He wasn't in a fit state to do anything and lay there, arms held over his head, moaning.

I heard Dad call out from the bushes.

'Did I get him?'

I went over and pulled him out.

'No Dad, you nearly hit me.'

He started laughing, then he looked down at the burglar and drew in a breath.

'He's hurt Tommy, go and get a glass of water.'

The bloke wasn't moving. I went inside, got the water, gave it to Dad and he threw it over the man, who opened his eyes and jumped.

I could see he was now scared.

'Alright, I've had enough,' he mumbled.

'You need to come in the house and get cleaned up,' Dad said.

He beckoned for me to pick the bloke up and bring him into the house.

I was confused. Five minutes ago he was trying to break in.

'Dad,' I said, 'he's just tried to burgle us.'

I didn't know what Dad had in mind, but I did as I was told and pulled the bloke to his feet. I half-carried, half-dragged him inside. There was blood all over his face and his top. One eye was already swollen shut.

We took him into the kitchen and sat him down. The bloke started shaking. I think he thought we were going to torture him.

'You look like you need a drink. Tea or coffee?' Dad asked him slowly.

The bloke looked confused.

'What are you going to do to me?' he stuttered.

'Tea ... or coffee?' Dad repeated slowly and purposely.

The bloke whimpered.

Dad sighed.

'Look, we're not going to hurt you. You need to sit there and calm down. You're in a bad way. Do you want tea or coffee?'

Meekly, the bloke asked for tea.

I was still confused. I couldn't understand why we were being nice to him.

Dad made him tea and then told me to go and get a flannel. I protested but I did as I was asked and Dad wiped the blood off his face.

Then he said, 'Go and get him a t-shirt, Tom. His top is ruined.'

*You're taking liberties now*, I thought as I went back upstairs to get a clean t-shirt to replace the ripped and bloodied one the man was wearing.

'Get him a hoodie as well,' Dad shouted after me.

Eventually the man was cleaned up, changed and drinking his tea. Dad started talking to him. He still looked worried but he realised by then that we weren't going to hurt him.

'So, what are you doing, trying to break into my house?' Dad asked.

Nervously, the man explained that he had been living rough and that he was an addict. He said he saw the house and the outbuilding and knew he could get £60 for a decent bike and £20 for a lawnmower.

'Why didn't you just knock on my door and ask for money?' Dad said. 'I would have given it to you.'

'I don't know you. No one does that anyway,' the bloke said.

Dad then opened a drawer in the kitchen where the cutlery was kept. The bloke jumped. He thought Dad was getting a knife. But Dad lifted the tray with the knives and forks in it and reached underneath where he kept a bit of money. He counted out a few hundred quid in cash.

He gave it to the bloke.

'Look mate, if you ever get in trouble again, don't go out thieving. We've all had hard times and been down, but you come and talk to someone, you come and talk to me. There's £200. Get yourself straight. Have you got somewhere to stay tonight?'

The bloke said he had and told Dad the address. We then walked him over the road to the bus stop and waited with him for a bus. When it pulled up, Dad put him on and told the bus driver not to let him off until he'd reached the address he said he was going to stay at.

The geezer looked at us and thanked us.

We walked back to the house, and I was still confused. I looked at Dad and said, 'Dad, what the fuck?'

'Listen,' he said, 'we've all had hard times, you smashed the fuck out of that poor bloke. He's got a problem. He's ill. If you can do a good deed and try to help someone out, it will come back for you one day.'

That was one hell of a way to teach someone a life lesson, but it was true. Years passed and it stuck with me because I've always tried to help people where I can.

There is a happy ending to this story. Much later, me and my dad were sitting outside The Ship having a drink. Dad had his vodka and slimline, I had a Stella. A geezer walked past, stopped, looked at us and walked on. He got about 100 metres up the road, stopped, turned around and came over to us.

*Who's this?* I was thinking.

He stopped in front of us and spoke to my dad.

'Sorry to bother you, but I just wanted to say something,' he started. 'A few years ago I broke into your house and your son beat the crap out of me. You took me in, washed me, helped me, made me a cup of tea, gave me some money and told me to get myself clean and sort myself out. That night I went to Queen's Hospital and admitted myself. I got help after that and since that day I've not touched a drug or a drink. I am working in Boots in Romford now. I have a bedsit as well. That day changed my life and I want to thank you and buy you a drink.'

I'm not ashamed to say it, that blew me away. The old man was right. A bit of kindness can change lives.

# SKINNER'S SCRIPTURES

- Everyone's good at something, find what you love and do that.

- Just because you're not a boffin, doesn't mean you are not smart.

- Exams aren't the be all and end all.

- Look for the opportunities in life and take them.

- Be a sponge and soak up knowledge.

- Be kind to people and don't judge until you know the full story.

# CHAPTER 3

# MATES ARE EVERYTHING

*'Happiness isn't measured by the amount of money in your pocket but by the wonderful people in your life.'*

HERE'S SOMETHING I truly believe. You can take over a country with a couple of good mates around you. Having a close group of friends who you can turn to when you are down, who you can support and most importantly who you can have a laugh with is one of the most important things in life.

I'm not a boffin by any stretch but I have heard that there are studies which show that people with a good circle of friends are happier than those who don't have lots of friends. I'm not sure how someone got funding to research that one to be honest. I mean, it's obvious. If you're out having a good time with your pals, you're going to be happier than Nobby No Mates sitting at home on his own with his meal for one and Netflix.

The lesson is: value your friends. Don't take them for granted.

Sometimes I think I must be the luckiest man in the world because I get to work with a lot of my mates, which means that every day is a laugh. I never get bored, and I always look forward to what the day has in store.

There is an important lesson there. Make friends with the people you work with because if you do, it's not like work anymore. We all have bad days at the office, right? We all have days where we just can't be bothered. Plenty of people are stuck in jobs they don't particularly enjoy but they have to be there because they need to earn a living. That sucks. But if you're in that position and you can have a laugh with the people you're with, or if you know that when the clock strikes five you can piss off down the pub with your colleagues and have a laugh, suddenly the job isn't such a chore.

In my world, mates and work often mix. Take Col, the black cab driver for example. I met him about four years ago. He gave me a lift and then he bought a bed from me and came to collect it in his black London taxi – the best taxis in the world.

Then there's Hughie, a personal trainer who I'd known for years from around Brentwood and who's now my partner in the gym that we own, Bosh Gyms. And there's Ross, the marketer who's like a 50-year-old businessman in a teenager's body. We met after *The Apprentice* and became good friends.

He took me to the British Grand Prix in Silverstone the first year it opened after Covid. He had a VIP marquee there for his clients, most of whom were multi-millionaire businesspeople, and then there was me at the end of the table, just buzzing about seeing the cars. At the time, I was planning to launch my own golf club, the Bosh driver. I had the idea to base the design on some of the most expensive clubs on the market, which I'd sent away to be analysed, but to make a competitor for a fraction of the retail cost.

I started chatting to a bloke about golf and explained about the clubs and how golfers were being ripped off.

'I bought one of those Cobra clubs which are a couple of hundred quid and sent it to a factory in China to see how much they could make a copy for,' I explained. 'They said they could do it for $25.'

He seemed really interested.

'All they are is a bit of metal and some fancy paintwork,' I continued.

When he asked me how I planned to market the clubs, I joked that the slogan would be 'like Cobra, but cheaper'.

'Anyway, what do you do?' I asked.

'I own the sports brand, Puma. We make Cobra golf clubs,' he said.

He was laughing thankfully and explained that he didn't think Bosh clubs were going to create too much competition for his company.

My mates are my support network and I always make sure I'm there for them. I ask them for advice when I need to, and we all talk to each other about personal things because that's 100 per cent important. Men can fall into the trap of keeping schtum and pretending everything's okay when times are tough, and that's not on. We should all be there for each other, and blokes shouldn't feel silly talking about emotions and personal stuff to each other. It's really important because there's a mental crisis among men. Suicide is the biggest cause of death in men under the age of 50 and around three quarters of deaths from suicides each year are men. Having a good network of friends and trusting that you can talk to your mates is one of the ways you can look after your mental health. We all need to be there for each other.

I've always been the glue that holds my mates together and if someone in my group of friends is depressed or having a hard time, I'll be there for them to help however I can, even if it's just to remind them that they're not alone and that the hard times won't last.

I know how important this stuff is, because one of my friends killed himself when I was younger and another mate shot himself. They were both in their early twenties. Another good mate was having a hard time and died in a car crash; no one knew whether it was an accident or on purpose. It made me realise that life is special and those around you could be gone tomorrow, so you should never take life or the people around you for granted. Don't sit around being miserable wishing you had stuff you haven't, it could all be gone tomorrow so make the most of what you have and celebrate it.

Losing a friend is devastating. Just after the pandemic another friend of mine died. Big Mark was an older guy and one of the people I used to turn to for advice. He was a lovely bloke and a larger-than-life character. He was a big Arsenal fan and loved the pub. We used to meet in The Archers in Romford and over the years he became a bit of a mentor to me. He'd done well for himself as a trader in the City and had a lovely family. I still miss him and his loss made me further appreciate how important mates are.

When you feel down or when you're going through a hard time, you can have counselling or go to therapy or go on a meditation course to find yourself. If that works for you, great. But I reckon having banter and a laugh with your mates is just as effective.

Someone once said to me, 'Tom, if I came to you and said I'd killed someone, you're the type of friend who would say, "Right, how many shovels do we need?"' I'm not sure that's true but I love the sentiment.

Friendship takes effort, but the reward is worth it.

It's probably a good point in the book to introduce you to some of my mates. These are some of the people who have been with me through thick and thin and who I work with and see every day. I've got lots of friends and there are loads of people I can't mention because, let's face it, it would be a shit book if most of it was just me listing my mates. But let me introduce you to a few of the people that I am lucky enough to be mates with.

## COLLINS

Born in Canning Town but now doing alright for himself in Brentwood, Collins works the markets and does the deliveries with me. He is like a trusty Transit van. He is dependable, loyal and a thoroughly decent bloke. All you have to do is feed him and water him and he'll never let you down. I've been up and down a million times in business and I would never have been able to get back on my feet without him.

I've known him for a long time. We were at school together and when the chips have been down, I've said to him, 'Look mate, this is going to be long and hard, there will be days when we are not going to want to get up, or we might not take any money, but we've got to trust each other and make it work.' And he's been right there with me. We both share the same mindset, that you can do anything if you put in the graft. Collins is hungry, he will put in a 19-hour day and not complain. There's been times when we've spent ten grand on stock, got up at 4 a.m. to drive to the market and worked all day but not taken a tenner. Days like that will crush most blokes. Collins just puts it behind him and starts again the next day. He's an optimist and a believer like me.

# BIG LANKS

Big Lanks is so-called because he's 6 ft 9 in tall and full of muscle. He's also covered in tattoos. I met him when I was 17, working on the markets and delivering mattresses out the back of the van.

I got a call from a bloke in Brentwood who bought a couple of beds from me. He liked them and mentioned that his mate was also looking for a mattress, so I said pass on my number. His mate was Big Lanks (people in my world rarely have proper names) who called a day later and put in his order. I told him I'd deliver the mattress on my way to playing golf the following day and pulled up outside his flat in the van wearing my golf outfit, which included a pair of brightly checked trousers. I looked like Rupert Bear.

I knocked on the door and this giant of a man came out. He'd obviously had a few drinks. He looked at me and said, 'Nice trousers,' then laughed.

'Thanks,' I replied, 'you look like a pisshead.'

We both started laughing. We knew it was just banter.

I helped him with the mattress, he paid, and I thought nothing more of it.

Two weeks later I was in a Brentwood nightclub. I was underage but I knew one of the doormen from the gym and he let me in. I was at the bar having a drink and a geezer came over to me and said, 'That mattress is fantastic.'

It was Big Lanks. We started having a chat and a laugh and had a few beers together. The doorman came over and started drinking with us and we ended up pulling two off-duty women police officers. We all went back to Big Lanks' place where he had a hot tub that we ended up in (it's Brentwood, what can I say, these things certainly aren't uncommon).

The ladies asked how Lanks and I met and Lanks told them that we were in the army together and that he was shot, wounded and stranded while on a mission. He said he collapsed in a trench in the desert, and called for an evacuation. According to his story, I was the one who was sent to rescue him.

'Tom came along with nothing but a shovel and a shotgun. He dug me out and saved my life. We've been best mates ever since,' he recounted. Of course, this was complete bollocks, but we carried on with that story for a long time afterwards. In fact, there will probably be a few people reading this who will be surprised to learn that neither me nor Lanks were in the special forces.

Later, we started working on the markets together and he did mattress deliveries for me when I had the bedding company. Because of the way he looked when he knocked on doors, people sometimes didn't answer because they were scared. They called the office and said there was a man knocking on the door who claimed to be from our company, but they didn't want to let him in.

'He's a very tall man covered in snake tattoos,' they'd say. We'd have to reassure them that it was okay, he was not a psychopath. He was our driver.

## LOU, KIM AND RYLAN

I knew sisters Lou (more about her later) and Kim when I was a kid, but they were a bit older than me and at the age of nine a few years is a big difference, so although we hung around in the same places and had the same circle of friends we weren't super close and drifted apart as we all went off and did our separate things. We reconnected many years later when I was running a handbag kiosk in Lakeside shopping centre and Kim walked past with her cousin, Rylan. Yes, *that* Rylan. She was a market trader too and sold women's clothing so we started talking and ended up working the markets together.

Kim is a grafter too and I'd often ring her on a Friday or Saturday night when I was out and ask her to keep a pitch for me at Dagenham Market the following day, because she was more sensible than me and would get up early, whereas I'd roll up later in the morning. We joined forces for a lot of deals and she became more like my big sister.

Through her I got to know Rylan well and we've had some blinding nights out together. Rylan is a lovely bloke. He was always going to be famous. When I first met him, he was a tall kid who wore a big set of sunglasses and had dyed golden hair and a little tash because he was only just growing facial hair. I met him just as he was about to go on Katie Price's modelling show, which was before he did *The X Factor*. Even before he was famous, he was a star. He had the personality. We used to go drinking with him in The Ship, and although on the face of it we are two very different people, we get on well and meet up regularly.

Last year Kim and Rylan, and me and my wife Sinéad went out for dinner and had a hilarious night. He's so recognisable that he gets stopped for selfies everywhere. It doesn't help that he's like 7 ft tall and always covered in bling. He doesn't do incognito. It was one of those nights where you can't stop laughing. At one point, we were in Little Italy in Soho and one of the waiters brought over a big bottle of champagne with sparklers on it and started singing 'Happy Birthday'. Rylan told them it was my birthday (it wasn't) and everyone in the restaurant got on their chairs and sung along. Later, when we were properly drunk, we facetimed Karren Brady.

We were in Soho, London, which is the gay centre of the UK and all of a sudden a big crowd of people clocked us and started shouting, 'OMG it's him, I love him!' Rylan laughed and said 'here we go' expecting to be mobbed. The crowd came over. 'Can we have a selfie, we're your biggest fans,' they were shouting. Rylan was very good-natured and prepared himself for a photo.

'No problem, of course you can,' he said. And with that they gave him the phone and crowded around me.

'We love you, Tom!' they were saying. Rylan saw the funny side of it.

# WARREN

I've known a lot of my closest friends since I was a kid at school, and although our lives have all taken different paths, when you've grown up in the same environment and had the same experiences, you share a bond. There's a line at the end of the movie *Stand By Me* where the main character says, 'I never had any friends later on like the ones I had when I was 12. Jesus, does anyone?'

It's true. Your early teenage years make you into who you are, and you have some of your best times when you are that young.

I've known Warren since school, so we go back years and I know his family well. His parents were wealthy, and when I was a teenager, they had a villa in Portugal in Quinta do Lago. We went out there for the whole summer when I was 16, my first lads' holiday, albeit with some parents in the background making sure we didn't get into too much trouble. I'd saved about a grand for the summer and dad gave me £500 to make sure I could pay my way. I'd been looking forward to it for months and by the time we landed I was like a kid in a sweet shop, excited about where to go first and what to do. We spent the first day at the beach and went mad at the water sports centre, hiring jet skis and going on the banana rides. In the evening, we went to an expensive place called Vale Do Lobo and had a meal. They didn't seem bothered about underage drinking, so it was easy to get served. We hit the cocktails and ended up in a club called The Gecko which was full of wealthy people from Surrey who had a few quid. We had more cocktails and I started ordering champagne. While we were there the band Kool & The Gang turned up. They must have been doing a gig in the area. We bought them drinks and they joined us at our table where we had a singalong with them. It was one of those mad unplanned nights and I was having the time of my life.

I don't remember much else but woke up the next morning with the worst hangover I ever had (the phrase we use in Essex is 'hanging out your arse', or 'hanging' for short). I looked in my wallet. I had 30 euros left.

Later in the day, I played golf with Warren's dad who'd heard us roll in during the early hours of the morning.

'Did you have a good night?' he asked, laughing.

'Yeah,' I said, 'but I've got a bit of a problem. I've run out of money,' I admitted.

'Mate, you're here another five weeks!' he reminded me.

I probably could have asked to borrow some funds from him and he would have agreed, but that wasn't the way I'd been brought up.

'Don't worry, I'll get a job,' I said.

I think he admired that and said that if I was serious, one of his mates had a bar and he would put in a word for me.

After golf he called his mate who agreed to see me, so I went for an interview and got a job in a Portuguese bar working twice a week. The money was enough to replenish my pot but the only problem was that the uniform was all white. I didn't have white shorts so Warren's dad, who was in his sixties, gave me a pair of his which were about ten sizes too big. He also lent me his push bike to ride to and from work. I didn't know how to speak Portuguese, but the bar was full of wealthy British people and I was going home with about 150 euros a night in tips. I was having it off and I came back home at the end of summer with more than I started. And me and Warren still had a great holiday.

## BEN THE BARBER

I met Ben when I was working as a Saturday boy in Just Gents barber shop in Gidea Park. I was 14, Ben was 18. He'd just come back from travelling and got a job cutting hair. As I got older we started hanging around and going out to the pub together and he became one of my best mates. He took me under his wing and got me into football and drinking and the party life.

He had a girlfriend called Tasha at the time and they were getting a place together in Romford. One year as her birthday was approaching, he asked for my opinion on what to get her. He wanted to buy her a vacuum cleaner and I laughed and told him not to be stupid and get her some perfume or something like that. He ignored the advice and bought her a Hoover. She left him.

A few years ago, before I'd settled down, I went on Ben's stag do to Ibiza. I was the youngest of the group at the time and so I was christened Little Tommy for the duration of the trip. Most of the activities were organised by Ben's best man, Big Bill. One day he booked us all on a party disco boat and before we set off, we met in the hotel bar where he pulled out a bag and announced that we were all going in costume as various superheroes. Ben was the female version of He-Man, She-Ra, or She-Man as we all called him, then there was The Hulk, Doctor Who, Batman, Superman and I got the Iron Man costume, complete with mask.

We got into our outfits and headed off to the boat where the party started. There was dancing and drinking and most of us were sweating our bollocks off in our suits but having a great time.

Now, I've never been into drugs. I love booze, but drugs never appealed to me. One of the stags came over to me and said, 'Tommy, do you want a pill?'

'No thanks', I answered. 'I've never taken one. I'm okay with the drink.'

But he wouldn't take no for an answer.

'You're in Ibiza Tommy, you've gotta.'

'They ain't for me,' I said.

'Just try one,' he said.

I gave in, took my first ecstasy pill and carried on dancing. Nothing happened.

'It's probably just a dud, have another one,' the 'dealer' explained 15 minutes later, as he handed me a baggie with about a dozen pills in it.

'I'll take two, just to make sure,' I said, and swallowed a couple.

I put my Iron Man helmet back on, carried on dancing and lost track of time. The sun started going down, the music was pounding, everything was beautiful. I looked around and grinned. I felt amazing. I was having the best time ever. I looked over at my mates and felt a profound surge of euphoric love for them. I was off my nut.

I suddenly had an urge to find Ben. I wandered around the boat until I found him and threw my arms around him.

'Ben, I fucking love you mate. Give me a cuddle. I'm so happy for you,' I said. I meant it. If I could have married him at that moment, I would have.

'I want to ring your wife and tell her how much I love you,' I babbled and then spent the next 15 minutes fixated on calling his wife-to-be. It was hard to get a signal because we were in the middle of the Med but eventually I got one bar and managed to get a connection.

'I love Ben,' I told her. 'This is the best day ever. He's the best bloke I've ever known.'

Things got a bit blurry after that, but I do remember climbing onto the roof of the boat's main cabin and sitting with my back against its funnel, watching the sunset while people below panicked and tried to coax me down.

When the party boat docked back in the marina, everyone dispersed in different directions and I found myself alone, wandering between Ibiza Town's bars and clubs, trying to find my mates.

At one door I was stopped by two bouncers.

'You can't come in here dressed as Iron Man,' they told me.

'I don't want to come in, I'm looking for my friends,' I explained.

'What do they look like?' they asked.

'Well, there's The Hulk, She-Man, Superman, Batman …' I tried to remember the full cast of characters. Then I turned around and saw Superman on the back of a rickshaw that was being driven by a dwarf.

'Don't worry, I've found one,' I said and trotted off after them. I'm sure the bouncers saw scenes like that every night.

That was the first and last time I've ever done drugs in my life.

# SKINNER'S SCRIPTURES

- Never take your mates for granted.

- Talk to each other and let your mates know you are there for them.

- Friendship takes effort, but the rewards are worth it.

- Iron Man must have been fucking roasting inside his suit.

# CHAPTER 4

# SKINNER'S HELPFUL INDEPENDENT TRADERS

*'The harder you work the luckier you get, and the luckier you get the more opportunities you get.'*

SOME PEOPLE CAN walk into a room where no one knows them and make everyone in there remember them when they leave. That can either be a skill or a curse, depending on what you are remembered for. The aim is to be remembered for the right reasons. 'What a lovely bloke he is,' rather than 'who invited that helmet?'

Not everyone has a natural ability to get themselves noticed. Not everyone finds it easy to talk to strangers and have a laugh. It is a skill that takes time to develop. Confidence is a big part of it. Some people call it having 'front'.

There's a fine line between being likeable because you can have a laugh and get on with people, and being an annoying Billy Big Bollocks, who people swerve when they see coming. People like a cheeky chappie; they don't like a dick. Learning the right balance is an important lesson in life. A lot of people try too hard and end up becoming annoying.

There are things in life that make us who we are. Environment makes us who we are, the places we grow up in, the places we live and the people we surround ourselves with. And also the places we work, particularly if you have the type of job that requires you to be a certain way. Cops, for example, all have certain common characteristics. So do builders and black cab drivers.

I'm the way I am because of my background and how and where I grew up, and also because of where I chose to work when I was younger. Markets made me who I am today, for better or worse.

I was about 14 when I first stepped foot on a market stall, and I never looked back. Growing up in Romford meant there was never a time when markets didn't play a part in my life. The market was the beating heart of the town. I was hooked from the start. I loved the hustle and bustle. Markets are full of life and the first time I stood behind a stall and started selling I felt like a king. I knew I was in the place I was supposed to be. It felt like home.

I first got a job early in the morning setting up a stall for a bloke called Nick the Greek who had a sweet shop and a stall in Romford market. Once you got known for setting up a stall for one trader, others asked too, because if they could get someone to set up for them at six in the morning, they got a lay in. I ended up doing several each weekend and used to get a fiver per stall to set them up and then take them down at the end of the day so the traders could piss off to the pub. It was a lucrative little job, and I could earn £20 to £30, which was a lot of money in those days for a teenager.

Markets were the centres of commerce for most towns I knew in those days. People went to the markets for entertainment on the weekend. Now they go to the mall, but back then you and your mates would trudge around the markets, looking for bargains. Just up the road from Romford was Dagenham Market, which has gone now but which used to be the biggest market in East London. It took place every Sunday and it sold everything from Nike tracksuits to CDs, three-seater sofas, wardrobes, number plates and doughnuts.

If you work in markets, you have to be reliable. You have to turn up when you say you will and you can't be afraid of early starts. That habit has stuck with me all my life. After I'd been setting up for a while, I started to get offers of day work, actually working in the stalls. I was naturally chatty and always had a laugh. I wasn't afraid of hard graft, and I guess some of the traders recognised that. I started working weekends on a men's clothing stall that mainly sold pants, socks, and t-shirts. I worked for an old boy there. He was in his late sixties and was an old-school trader. He'd been doing it all his life and you could tell it was in his blood. He had all the patter and he used to talk all day. It was like watching a performance. He'd switch on as soon as the punters arrived. A lot of what he said was random bollocks, but it made people laugh and it drew in the customers. He used to make up riddles and I never understood what he was going on about, no one did, but it didn't matter.

'Barry's me uncle and that's why he's got the t-shirt. Me auntie Audrey, she bought a strawberry. £3 for a pound. Come and have a look, I'm wearing a crown.'

I learned a lot from watching him because people loved him. It was like he was a character, larger than life and funny. If you make people laugh you make them relaxed, and when they're relaxed they are more likely to buy from you. He was always laughing. I never saw him get annoyed or down, and even when he had a tricky customer, or some-one who was rude, he had a knack of either making them laugh eventually, or taking the piss out of them so everyone else laughed at them. He was a clever bloke. He knew how to work the crowd.

Eventually I started running my own stall at Dagenham Market on Sundays which I used to stock with bric-a-brac and seconds that I got hold of, like the hoodies that hadn't got hoods on them which I sold for a couple of quid each. My dad had a handbag business at the time, and I bought all the damaged ones off him, like the ones where the zip didn't work. They went for a fiver.

You go on the market to learn life. In my opinion, it's such a loss that markets are dying out now, because you could teach kids a lot by sending them to work on a market stall. A lot of my mates worked weekends on market stalls too when they were teenagers and none of them suffer from anxiety or any of the other problems that teenagers seem to have nowadays. You can't hide on a market stall. You have to come out of your shell. I always think it's a shame that I started working on markets when I did and not twenty years before in the eighties when you could really make a fortune as a trader.

My first proper business venture was a market stall and it's an area of business I've returned to repeatedly over the years because it's my natural environment. I never had a set product. I sold whatever I could get for a good price, so it was always something different every week. By the time I was 17, I was proudly driving a white Mercedes Sprinter van with the words Skinner's Helpful Independent Traders written in a column down the side with the first letter of each word in bold. Underneath this I had the words New York, Paris, Romford.

I learned on the job. I learned that a decent stall needs to have 30 or 40 different lines at different price points. You have your low-margin stock that you sell cheaply and quickly. You sell 150 and they make £1 profit each, that's £150. Then you have your mid-price stock. You sell 50 of them and they make you a fiver each, that's £250. Then you have your high-margin items that you aim to sell the most of. Say they make you £12 profit per item. If you sell 100, that's £1,200. Add it all up and you've made £1,600. Out of that come your costs. Some markets charge £200 a day for a stall while others can be £60 or £70 a day, depending on the size of the pitch and where you are. Then you have to factor in footfall. The top markets were North Weald and

Bovingdon. Both were dear. Out of London they were some-times cheaper. Worthing was £40. Sometimes you could make more money setting up a stall at one of the big car boot sales. The lessons I learned on the markets were the same kind of lessons that apply to any kind of business: supply and demand, marketing, building a customer base. It all applies equally whether you are selling cheap shower gel or luxury cars.

After several years, I knew markets inside out and so well that it was almost like I'd developed a sixth sense. I usually knew what would sell and what wouldn't. There's no point buying a pallet load of out-of-date 'I Love Harry and Meghan' wedding celebration biscuits, for example, no matter how blinding the deal is, because people won't want them. It takes years of experience to spot something that will sell and to be honest, I still get it wrong sometimes. We all do. Sometimes you're certain something is a winner, and you dive in, and by the time you realise you've bought a dud, it's too late. One of the worst mistakes you can make is to buy things for yourself, rather than for the general public. You need things that everyone uses, or that are a little bit of luxury at an affordable price. One of my worst buying decisions involved half a lorry load of laughing monkeys.

On reflection, I reckon I was blindsided by them because when I bought them I wasn't a parent, so I didn't appreciate just how fucking annoying they were.

The story started with me and Big Lanks working a stall in Bovingdon Market, which took place on a disused airfield in Hemel Hempstead, Hertfordshire every Saturday. It was a massive market and a good earner if you had the right stock. We were there in November, so it was the run up to Christmas, which is peak market season and we were doing very nicely when a geezer came up to the stall for a chat about some lines he had to sell.

This is common practice in markets. Other traders will often be sniffing around to see what they can sell and what's on offer.

So, this bloke explains to us that he's got some lines that he's looking to get rid of for a bargain price. I can't remember what they all were, but when he said 'laughing monkeys' my ears pricked up.

'What the fuck are laughing monkeys?' I asked.

He explained that they were kids' toys. They were fluffy monkeys in a box, and they had motion sensors in them so whenever someone walked past them, they laughed. He showed me a photo on his phone. They looked just like he described them, cartoon monkeys in a box with a big grin on their mugs.

'They're from Hamleys,' he explained. 'They retail at £29.99, you can have them for £3 each.'

I thought back to my childhood and wondered if I would have liked a laughing monkey when I was a kid. I reckoned I would.

'Why are they so cheap?' I asked.

The bloke got a bit cagey.

'They had too many in stock, they over-ordered and couldn't sell them,' he mumbled.

I turned to Lanks.

'What do you think, £6 each, two for a tenner? Gotta be worth a go just before Christmas.'

'I'll be honest with you Tom,' he answered, 'who's gonna buy a monkey that laughs?'

'For the kids,' I said, 'they'd make nice stocking fillers.'

To be fair to Lanks, he had kids, so he knew more about that sort of stuff than I did.

'My kids wouldn't want one,' he sniffed.

I looked at the bloke.

'How many have you got?'

'Two thousand five hundred of them,' he said.

Lanks was shaking his head.

'Tom, you're on crack, they ain't gonna sell,' he warned.

I did a quick calculation of the profit we could make.

'Lanks, I ain't listening to you, I'm buying 'em.'

I turned to the bloke.

'We'll have 'em,' I said, and held out my hand to shake. The deal was done. We were now the proud owners of 2,500 laughing monkeys for £7,500, just in time for Christmas. We had several markets lined up for the following weeks and I could see pound signs in my eyes. Every kid around London would wake up that Christmas morning to the sound of a laughing monkey, I was sure of it.

The bloke went to get the parcel (that's what we call a consignment of stock), and we made space on the stall for the first batch. The rest would go in the van ready to be sold in the following weeks.

I lined up about 20 in the front of the stall, pride of place so anyone passing could see them. I realised straight away that it didn't matter where they went, you couldn't miss them because as soon as someone moved, they started laughing, and it wasn't a pleasant chuckle. These things cackled really loudly, and because the market was busy, they didn't stop.

I tried to shout above the din.

'Come on, ladies and gentlemen! Just in time for Santa. Get your laughing monkeys, £6 each, two for a tenner. Every good kid deserves one!'

People were stopping and looking, then frowning and walking away.

I heard a few comments.

'What's that fucking awful noise!'

They were right. These things sounded demonic. After an hour they were driving us mad. Lanks was walking around shaking his head and tutting. I realised why they were taken off the shelves in Hamleys. The kids must have been scared shitless.

During that whole day I managed to sell maybe a handful and we packed the rest up in the van with all the others at the end of the day. As we drove back home, they were in the back, laughing at us.

'Don't worry mate,' I said to Lanks. 'It's early days, we'll shift them.'

I went to bed that night with the sound of laughing monkeys ringing in my ears.

Over the following weeks we lugged them from market to market and it was the same story at each. They sat on the stall, howling away. People would tell us how awful they sounded. I thought about trying to turn them off, or taking out the batteries but that was even worse. How could you sell a laughing monkey that wasn't laughing? I felt sorry for anyone who had the misfortune of being on a stall next to us. I'd shrug apologetically as the din started up and my stock literally went apeshit. It sounded like one of those scenes in a nature documentary when a troop of apes start fighting and screaming at each other.

I started to hate those laughing monkeys, they haunted me. The price eventually came down to a pound. I just wanted rid of them but still no one was buying.

Christmas came and went and I had maybe sold a few hundred. They were dud stock and they went to the warehouse where they stayed for several months in the corner of shame while I tried to work out what to do with them. I knew I was never going to be able to recoup the money I'd spent on them and I ended up giving them to a charity shop about six months later. I can't remember which one, but it should have been one for the hard of hearing.

It wasn't until a few years later that I started going to Dino's and I reckon if I'd have asked anyone in there at the time whether 2,500 laughing monkeys was a good idea, they would have warned me off ... or laughed at me.

So, what's the moral of the story? Everyone makes mistakes and even when you are 100 per cent sure you're right, you can be wrong. Listen to people and take advice and most importantly, if something seems too good to be true, it usually is. Oh, and if someone offers you a pallet of laughing monkeys, tell them where to go.

Laughing monkeys aside, I got good at reading the runes. I could tell by the weather, the location and the time of year whether we were going to have it off and nick a few quid or whether we'd be packing up early and loading most of the stock back on the van.

Not so long ago I was on a market in St Albans with Collins just days before Christmas. The Luton van was full to the brim with stock, mostly pillows as at the time I had a pillow company. We got to the market at 5.30 a.m. and the weather was awful, it was sleet and snow, freezing cold and dark. We were wearing fingerless gloves, long johns, two pairs of tracksuit bottoms, coats and hoodies. The ground was wet and the boxes of stock were getting soggy. It wasn't a great start and Collins was convinced we were going to have a crap day. I, on the other hand, had a feeling that it was going to be a blinder.

Soon after we set up my phone rang. I answered. It was a liquidator I knew who was offering me a deal on a van load of liquidated stock he wanted to get rid of before Christmas.

'I have some fantastic lines Tom and it's a good price, but the deal is you have to buy everything, you can't pick and choose,' he said.

He listed what he had. It was all stuff that would make good Christmas gifts: toys, kids' bikes, scooters, massage guns, that sort of stuff. All random, but all things people would buy at the right price.

This particular day, I hadn't done the markets for a while, and we didn't know how it was going to work out, but I had a feeling it was going to be a good day. I had faith and confidence. I'm the first to admit that I'm not a good businessman, there is lots I don't know, but one thing I am is a people person, and I'm a hard worker and I can sell, and I was certain that I could work some of the old market magic and sell this stock, so I told him we'd have it.

Half an hour later the bloke turned up with half a lorry load of gear and it was good stuff. There were kids' bikes that retailed at £50, massage guns that would have sold in the shops for £70, all kinds of treasures. Collins wasn't sure. He was shaking his head. Two things were worrying him. Firstly, Christmas was just a week away and if we didn't sell the stuff there and then we'd be lumbered with it for months, and secondly, I had just given my warehouse back so I had nowhere to put it if we couldn't shift it.

'What are you going to do if we can't sell it today?' he asked.

'Don't you worry mate, we're going to sell it all today. And if we don't, we'll just leave it here.'

'So you're risking all the money we've built up?' he said.

'I'll make it happen,' I reassured him.

'I fucking love you, Tom,' he said, shaking his head.

We unloaded the stock and piled it up around our stall. We were next to a bus stop and we stored some of the boxes in there as well. There were boxes stacked 8 ft high around us. It was like a warehouse on the market. By 9 a.m. we were ready to go and it was still raining. The boxes were getting wet, there was no one there. I could see the look on Collins' face.

'We're going to have a good day,' I reassured him.

At that point in my life, I had already started using social media a bit and I tweeted a post to say that we had some blinding Christmas bargains on offer.

At 9.30 a.m. the clouds parted and the sun came through. It was like something from a film. This beam of sunshine shone down directly onto our stall and people started to turn up almost from out of nowhere. We turned into selling monsters. We couldn't keep track of the amount of punters we had. By mid-morning we ran out of carrier bags and I had to order 1,000 more to be delivered to us that day. It was non-stop. We didn't stop for a cup of tea or a sandwich. At the end of the day the market shut and everyone else packed up, but we stayed where we were and carried on. I ran into Robert Dyas across the road and bought two big lights which we set up so we could carry on selling. It got to about 7 p.m. and there were people dressed up in their party gear going to Christmas parties while we were still there selling. I looked around and there was hardly anything left, just a couple of boxes.

'I think we'll call it a day,' I said.

We had a bag full of money like you wouldn't believe. Collins turned to me and said, 'Tom, you've made my Christmas.'

Having the right stock is one of the golden rules. It also helps to have a jingle or a slogan. A while back I was on a stall with Lanks and had a load of moisturiser that was packed up similar to Olay cream, but wasn't. We made up a little song and were singing it all day. '*Ole, Ole is the voice you'll hear, when the boys from Romford are gone from here. This Ole cream is all half price, but if you buy today it's twice as nice.*'

We were singing along when a woman came over and said, 'I use Olay every day from Boots and that doesn't look like the Olay that I buy.'

'Of course it isn't,' I said, 'because it's on a market stall and you can buy three for a fiver.'

She asked to smell it and as she put her nose to the top of the tube Lanks squeezed it. It creamed all over her face. I was crying with laughter.

That's the thing with market traders. You always have a laugh, and you tend to get away with murder if you do things with a smile and a glint in your eye. There's a real community and everyone helps each other.

When I started out, I was quite young for a trader and several of the older guys took me under their wing and helped me learn the ropes. People like Pete and Alex who are Dino's regulars and always have a word of advice.

Pete said I reminded him of the kind of trader you would see back in the eighties working down Oxford Street, in London. He says there were a few fellas there who never failed to get money. They used to sit on a milk crate or box and sell all day every day.

Alex is like the wise man of the markets. He steered me in the right direction and a lot of the stock I sold came through him. He's got his own food company and a good knowledge of the trade and good contacts. When I first started on the markets, he gave me some credit to get me started with a bit of stock.

One year he offered a parcel of toiletry gift boxes. They had soap, shower gel and a moisturiser. They looked like £50 worth, and they retailed for about £30 online. He was offering a pallet load of them for £8 each.

'Sell them for a tenner and you will sell hundreds,' he said.

'They're only £8, there's not a lot of money in them,' I replied.

But Alex was a trading guru so I took his advice and we put them out on the stall and sold 200 in a day. He understands how to price things and it's a lesson he taught me. As another example, several years ago I bought some wooden Winnie the Pooh toys and they were beautiful but individually on the stall no one would pick them up. Instead, I did a multibuy deal selling five sets that would have retailed at £100 for £20.

'Come have a look, save yourself £80, it's only a score!'

People queued up because once they knew they were getting a bargain, they couldn't resist. No one wants to be first to buy but once they put their toe in the water, they all want to get in on the act. Everyone loves a bargain and if you get enough bargains and enough decent stock to sell you get known as someone who sells quality stuff and the customers come back every week to see what you have. That's how I developed a reputation, although I didn't always stay in one place.

Look after your customers and they look after you. That's one of the golden rules of market trading. I think sometimes there's an unfair view that market traders are out to fleece people and that markets are these dodgy places where no one can be trusted and everything on sale will fall apart in a week. That's totally wrong. Market people are salt of the earth, and their value to communities is often overlooked. When people fall on hard times, or when prices go up like they have done in the last few years, people need bargains and markets have traditionally been the places they've found them.

It makes me angry sometimes when I turn up at some markets and see how neglected these once thriving places have become.

We were in Worthing Market not so long ago and all the traders had been moaning about the state of the paving for ages, but the council was doing nothing about it. There were loads of loose slabs that people were tripping over. All the council had done was put a few cones out to try and warn people.

There were a couple of loose slabs in front of our stall and all day I was constantly having to warn people. Mums couldn't get their buggies past and one lady tripped over, fell flat on her arse and hurt her elbow. Luckily, I was out the front of the stall when a second lady, who must have been in her eighties, tripped. I managed to save her. It was a freezing cold day and if she'd hit the floor, I don't know what would have happened to her. Falls finish off old people. I got so annoyed about it that I called up the council and had a go at them. They happily take a fee from market traders for rent, the least they could do was create a safe environment for people. I told them they needed to fix it asap before someone really got hurt. They replied with the usual red tape. *It's been like that for years. We haven't got the funds. We need to get approval from the committee.* I told them all they needed to do was muck up a bit of concrete and re-lay the paving.

'It will take 30 seconds,' I told them. But no, the works department needed to get a budget signed off from the committee, or something like that.

I believe that if there's a job to do, you should just get it done. You don't need to have meetings. Just get out there and do it. And with that attitude, later that day, me and Collins popped to B&Q, bought a bag of cement and fixed the paving ourselves.

I'm not going to completely sugar coat the market experience and make out like everyone is a saint, because they aren't. You get dodgy people in markets the same as you get dodgy people everywhere in life. But even the dodgy people have a code. Market traders won't stitch up other traders and traders will close ranks to protect each other.

That's not to say you shouldn't be on your toes if you decide to dip your toe in the world of market trading. I've had plenty of close shaves on stalls. I remember one Christmas when I was doing a line of running sets that were selling like hot cakes. You got a running jacket, a water bottle with a handle, a stopwatch and a pair of running socks. I was knocking them out for £30 when they would have retailed at £60 and I was ''aving it off', as the saying goes. In those days I had a zip-up money belt that I kept my takings in, which were mainly cash. I was on my own at the stall that day and about midway through a bloke came over to the front of my stall with a carrier bag and he ushered me over.

'I'm working bruv, leave me alone,' I said.

He was insistent. He spoke in a heavy Irish accent.

'Come here and look what I've got. You'll want a bit of it.'

He wasn't going to go away so I walked over to him. He opened the bag to show me it was packed full of tobacco and cigarettes.

'£2 a pouch, cigarettes £3 a box,' he said, his eyes darting around shiftily.

I followed his gaze and in the corner of my eye I saw three or four younger guys grabbing the boxes of stock from the back of my van which was parked next to the stall. Classic distraction technique.

'Thief!' I yelled.

Immediately several of the neighbouring traders started shouting at them and ran out from behind their stalls to help.

The crooks knew that the other traders would be unforgiving, so they dropped the gear and legged it. Quick as a flash I turned to the guy in front of me and gave him a clump, to put him off trying the same trick on someone else. He dropped to the ground, got up and ran off after his mates. As he did he turned and yelled a threat.

'Wait and see what you're going to get,' he called.

*Great*, I thought, *I'm now stuck on a stall that I can't leave, I'm alone and my van is blocked in and I have a fat bag full of cash.*

I carried on working and at the end of the day I'd sold out my stock and had several grand in cash in the money belt which I emptied and stuffed in the glove compartment.

As it happened, I had a cold and a runny nose that day, so as I was taking down the stall I was blowing my nose and putting the tissues in the belt. I also jammed my gloves in it.

I was the last to leave and as I broke down the last bits of the frame, I saw six or seven blokes marching up the aisle towards me with an older man in the middle holding the wrist of the bloke I'd given a slap. I knew what they'd come for. They'd waited until no one else was around.

The old man came up to me, put his finger on my chest and pushed me backwards.

'Why did you hit a good honest man?' he asked, also in a broad Irish accent. 'This man was out here selling and grafting, just like you, and you attacked him.'

I laughed.

'Don't be a mug, he was distracting me so his little mates could rob my stall,' I told him.

'That's not what he tells me,' the man said.

'Well, he's lying to you, he tried to swerve me away from my stall.'

I could see the old bloke thinking it over. I recognised some of the others as the blokes who had tried to take the stock.

'Those wankers were with him,' I said.

The old man, who was obviously the leader of this band of crooks, made up his mind.

'You hurt him and he wants some money for compensation,' he said. 'You had a good day, you need to pay for what you did to him.'

I wasn't going to be bullied and was ready to fight to keep my takings if need be.

'You ain't having no money,' I said.

He thought about this and came up with what I assume he thought was a face-saving solution for both sides.

'Are you a gambling man?' he asked.

I nodded yes.

'Okay, fair bet,' he said. 'The toss of a coin, you win and you walk away without a scratch on your head and you keep everything you got. I win and you hand over the money belt with every penny in it.'

'This money belt here?' I said, gesturing at the belt that was hanging around my waist.

'That one there,' he said.

'Okay,' I agreed. 'It's a deal.'

With that he pulled out a pound coin and flipped it in the air. The goons with him watched with grins on their faces as it spun through the air. I called heads and it came down tails. They all cheered. I sighed dramatically, unclipped the belt and gave it to the man who was looking pleased with himself.

And then he opened it up to reveal a scrunched-up wad of snotty tissues and a pair of gloves.

'Shame,' I said, 'I liked those gloves.'

The look on his face was priceless, but he knew a deal was a deal and to his credit he shook my hand and laughed too.

'I'll be seeing you soon,' he said as he turned and walked off, which I suppose was meant to be some kind of threat but didn't bother me.

I never did see him again thankfully and when I went back the following week, I kept an eye out for any more thieves, but they must have learned their lesson and moved on. In hindsight I had been outnumbered and outgunned but even among thieves there's a code of honour.

# SKINNER'S SCRIPTURES

- Listen to people who know more about something than you do.

- Don't base all your decisions on your own personal opinions.

- We all fuck up. When you do, learn from it and move on.

- If there's a job that needs doing, do it.

## CHAPTER 5

# THE ART OF THE DEAL

*'You can either have 100 per cent of fuck all,*
*or 50 per cent of something.'*

PEOPLE OFTEN ASK me for business advice because I'm a grafter and because I was on *The Apprentice*. I usually tell them this: 'Mate, you're asking the wrong person, I'm not a good businessperson.' And that's the truth. I'm not. I've been up and down a hundred times and I've had businesses that have done well, and businesses that haven't. I'm not good at all on the background stuff that makes people good at business. I'm not great at managing money, I hate meetings, I don't do much planning or strategising. I don't have a five-year plan. I've rarely got a one-year plan beyond going on holiday and making enough to pay the rent and treat the family. So no, I'm not that good at business. But what I am good at is making money. That's where I think I can confidently offer some advice, if you are interested. I know some people will be saying, 'But Tom, business is all about making money.' They're right. A big part of it is. But there is a lot more to business and there are a lot of successful businesses that don't actually make lots of money.

The reason I'm good at making money is that I'm good at doing deals. From those first days on the markets, I've always loved the chase of the deal. I get a buzz from negotiation, from trying to get a good price when buying stock, from trying to get the money down from the supplier but not squeezing them so tight that they'll never do business with me again. I like working out what I can sell the stock for, and whether what I am buying is going to sell or not.

It's a skill that I learned over time. When I was younger and first started out trading, I used to buy everything I was offered like an enthusiastic puppy and half of it wouldn't sell, but as I got older I got wiser and started to understand a bit about market economics. People like to know they are getting a bargain, but you can't just sell them crap, because they'll never come back. This is a lesson in life too. It doesn't just relate to goods; it relates to services and to personality too. If you want people to engage with you, make them like you. Be good to them, be kind, just be a decent person. Don't be a laughing monkey. Be useful, make yourself useful.

I've always found I get on with people. I never argue and if I'm not happy with something or someone I'll usually just walk away (unless I'm threatened). Life is too short to hold grudges and I've always found that people who go round upsetting others and being argumentative don't get far in life. As the saying goes, you catch more flies with honey than you do with vinegar.

The way I see it, negotiation is a bit of a game and everyone is bluffing each other, but in a good-natured way. If someone is selling me something, I try to give the impression I don't want it, but when I'm selling the same product, having bought it from the person who I told I didn't want it, it's the best thing in the world. The simple rule is: best thing in the world when you are selling, load of shit when you are buying.

That said, when I'm negotiating, I'm always aware that everyone has to earn a pound note, and although I'll try and get the best price, I won't take the Mickey and try and screw someone into the ground. That's bad business and it's unfair. It happens too often to smaller suppliers who get contracts with big retailers and find that the big boys ratchet down the prices so much that it becomes impossible to make a living. Just ask anyone who owns a farm and has a contract to supply a big supermarket.

It's better if you all make a quid and you can all eat at the end of the day. If you are the sort of person who batters people down on price all the time, eventually they'll stop doing business with you, or you'll put them out of business. You can either have 50 per cent of something, or 100 per cent of fuck all. Little and often is the key.

And the upside of being reasonable is that when people like doing business with you, they tend to stick with you. I haven't studied it, but I would bet that there is a direct relationship between people who are decent when it comes to business and people who get a lot of business opportunities.

Generally in life, if you make lots of contacts, if you chat to people, if you are fair to people, if you are nice to people, if you can have a laugh with people, and if you keep your eyes open, there will always be something around the corner.

That philosophy has done me well and is probably why I know loads of people who I can deal with and who will deal with me. Some of them are acquaintances, some of them are friends. Some of them started out as business acquaintances and became friends.

Doing good deals is about knowing what people want, being able to talk to people, being genuine and being fair with people. You'll find loads of business books that go into loads of details and that break it all down into scientific theories, like you've got be more like a chimp, or you've got to be a psychopath, and to be honest I haven't read them so they might be brilliant, but in my life, that's how I operate, and it seems to work. So much so that if I suddenly found myself with the urgent need to find several thousand by tomorrow, I probably could, although I'd struggle to find it the day after.

It took a few years to learn this lesson. When I was starting out in business properly in my late teens and early twenties, I was a rough diamond and the environment I hung around in wasn't exactly your Harvard Business School. I had my trusty van, my market stalls and gradually worked up until my portfolio included the static stall in Lakeside which, in my opinion, was the jewel in my business empire, mainly because it was indoors and there was a food court five minutes' walk away.

I sold everywhere and I sold everything, even on a Sunday when most people were relaxing with the *EastEnders* omnibus, a pint and a roast dinner. I was out making money. That was my church, doing a deal. One of the best places to knock out stuff back then was the all-important New Inn. I loved the place and still have great memories of it, even though it was a bit of a shit hole. What made it so great were the people in it, rather than the décor, which wasn't up to much. More Benson & Hedges than Farrow & Ball. It was in Romford, but it was like a proper East End pub. They used to sell shellfish there, proper stuff like cockles and whelks, and they put free roast potatoes on the bar for punters which were so salty and crispy they made your lips go numb. It was a clever trick because you thought you were getting something for nothing, but after two potatoes you needed a pint to quench your thirst from all the salt.

On a Sunday it was always buzzing and Kim and I used to go there after Romford Market and do clothes parties, which involved setting our gear out on a table. Kim would have faux fur, women's tracksuits and that kind of stuff and I'd have things like candles and handbags. Once we'd set up, I'd go and get a pint and a bottle of white wine and we'd stay there for the rest of the day. We'd sell loads of stuff because the blokes in the pub would buy presents for their wives and partners so they could stay out later drinking: 'guilt gifts' we used to call them. We always did well in the New Inn, but drank half the profits throughout the day.

And that brings me to one of the reasons why I say I'm not a good businessperson. I'm good at making money, but I'm even better at spending it. Things changed more when I had a family and I became a bit more sensible, but I've always been someone who enjoys spending money and back in those days when I had no responsibilities, if I had it I spent it.

Kim often reminds me of the night we went out and I had to stop and get the takings from the shut-up stall in Lakeside, which was about £5,000. We went into the Sugar Hut and by the next day I'd blown the lot, buying everyone drinks and throwing my cash around, giving it large.

This carelessness sometimes got me into trouble. I liked having a good time and sometimes took my eye off the ball. Like the time I went up to my mate's apartment to watch the football and have a beer and left my van parked outside his flat with thousands of pounds of stock in the back. I should have unloaded it into the warehouse I had at the time, but I was running late and didn't want to miss the kick-off.

I was 19 and doing well for myself. I had a nice van and every week what I earned on the market I inevitably blew on Saturday and Sunday in Mayfair buying bottles of

Laurent Perrier Rosé like an idiot. This particular week I'd been sensible, however, and I bought a parcel of designer coats which I knew would sell well. There were about 500 of them, so it was a big deal. All my money was tied up in them, but I got them for a steal. They were about £150 in the shops, and I got them from a liquidator for £30 each. I did the figures and reckoned I could make around £25,000 in the couple of weeks it would take me to sell them.

With all my business equity in the back of the van, I locked it up and went upstairs to watch the game. We cracked open a couple of beers and after ten minutes I fancied a cigarette and realised I'd left a packet in the van, so I went back down to get them.

The flat was on North Street, Romford, which wasn't the nicest part of town, so in hindsight I shouldn't have been that surprised when I walked out onto the street to find the van had gone. I did that thing for a couple of seconds where I stood there looking up and down the road, confused and trying to work out if I'd forgotten where I parked it. But I was definitely in the right place and the van had definitely gone. For a split second I hoped maybe it had been towed away, but there were no parking restrictions and given the area I was in, I knew the reality. It had been nicked, along with all my stock.

*For fuck sake, how's me luck*, I thought to myself. This was a major business setback. I had no money to buy any more stock or another van and if I wanted to earn my way out of the predicament, I needed a van to work. I was too young to rent one because you had to be over 23.

Out of desperation I did something I never did, and I went to Dad to ask if he would loan me a couple of grand to see me through until I could recoup my losses, which I knew I could.

Dad decided it was time for me to learn an important lesson.

'But I thought you'd been doing well for yourself,' he said when I asked for the money. 'You've been giving it Larry Large up the West End telling everyone how much you earn. Where's your money?'

'I've spent it all,' I admitted.

'What an idiot you are then, this'll teach you a lesson.'

Needless to say, he didn't put his hand in his pocket for me.

I asked another mate too, who I'd bought the van from, but he laughed and wondered why anyone would nick 'that heap of old shit'.

It was a tough lesson to learn, but I made the money back through graft. I never felt sorry for myself or panicked, and I never once thought of giving up. It was a case of starting again and building things up, which I'd done before and which I've done since. I did learn and after that I did start to get a bit more responsible and put some money aside regularly, so I had a bit of a cushion when emergencies arose. I still enjoyed spending however, because let's face it, what's the point of money if you can't enjoy it. Money's never been my God in that respect. I enjoy the things it brings and allows me to do, but I don't worship it.

Over the years I became known as the man who could get you anything, anywhere. I had contacts and could get watches, Moncler jumpers, Ugg boots. Were they snide? I don't know, I'm not a fashion designer, I'm not a jeweller. All I know is that no one complained.

I developed an intuition for spotting a deal and working out the margins. I got a warehouse full of liquidated branded toiletry gift sets one year and sold 12,000 of them, 200 a day every day for 60 days. There was only a couple of quid profit in each, but it was good money. Pillows were always good sellers, and I found a supplier who sold them at £2.30 for two. I sold them for £5 for two and could get rid of several hundred a day. However, I was limited as to how many I could sell because they took up a lot of room in the van. I could only take 400 out at a time. That gave me around £1,000 profit, which sounds like a lot for a day but didn't work out so good after costs for the pitch, diesel and a bit of lunch were considered.

I started working in markets just as they began to decline. They were still buzzing in the nineties when people could sell their pitch in Romford Market for a hundred grand, but the heyday, when you really could do deals and make fortunes, was the eighties. That's not to say they don't have their place today. There are still good markets out there, but now people tend to sit in their front rooms on a laptop or iPad and order cheap stuff which arrives the next day from a faceless business they have no connection or loyalty to. We've swapped convenience for the joy of getting out and about and connecting with the things we buy and the people we buy them from. We don't touch what we buy, feel it, smell it or look at it anymore. When you think about it, how mad is it that we buy things like aftershave and perfume without even smelling it. Or fruit and veg from a website that we only see when someone delivers it. That's the thing I love about trading, you have something physical that you can see and touch. There is no emotional attachment with buying anymore. Perhaps that is why we buy so much. It's easier to make something look good on a computer screen.

Anyway, I learned how to do deals through experience. I was never one for business books and business courses. I learned my sales skill in the school of life and I have never been what you'd call a conventional businessman, or a conventional salesperson. I hate meetings. I don't wear a suit very often and I hate being in an office. I'm happiest on the road, in my van, or on a stall where I can talk to people. I did have an office once when my bed business expanded, but being there all the time and going to meetings did my head in.

I can't sit still in that kind of environment. I think it's my dyslexia. I can't focus for long periods of time. People talk lots of shit in the business world.

By the time I was in my thirties, I'd learned a lot and been up and down many times, but to be honest, none of it is rocket science. The art of business is to have small overheads and large profits. That's what any good business needs.

Now I do things on intuition. I'm a big believer in doing things on a whim and striking while the iron's hot. If opportunity knocks, open the door.

A classic story to illustrate this is the story of how I started my gym, Bosh Gyms. I went into partnership with a guy I know called Hughie, who trains boxers. We knew each other from around Brentwood and I met him in a pub one night and mentioned that I was thinking about doing some training and maybe taking part in a boxing match, because I used to box when I was younger and enjoyed it.

The next morning at 5 a.m. I was on the khazi checking my phone and Hughie was doing the same. He saw I was online and messaged me to say why don't I meet him at the gym for a session. That was on Monday. By Wednesday he'd arranged a fight for me and by Friday we'd bought a gym together, which we gutted and refitted and opened three weeks later.

I've tried my hand at lots of ideas and businesses but the one thing that's always bailed me out is my ability to sell.

I'll finish with a story about one of the best deals I ever did. It was soon after I'd been on *The Apprentice* and through the show I met a couple of American businessmen who owned a bicycle company. They were involved in one of the tasks on the show and during filming we got on well. They were so impressed by my sales patter that after filming they contacted me and made me an offer.

On the show, I genuinely sold £100,000 of their products and they admitted that they'd never sold that much before in a single deal.

They called me and explained that they had a stand at a big bicycle accessories show in Germany near the Italian border.

'We'll give you $15,000 if you come out and be our salesman for the weekend,' they offered.

I didn't have to think about it and said yes straight away. What an opportunity. Even if I sold nothing, I still walked away with a decent pay packet for a weekend's work and they were covering my expenses. I was looking forward to trying out some German beers while I was there too. I was confident that I'd be able to sell some of their products as I knew about cycling, having spent most of my childhood pedalling around Romford.

The exhibition turned out to be a big deal. There were accessory manufacturers and bicycle retailers from all over the world there in a huge exhibition centre. I flew out to meet the Americans the afternoon before the event started and straight away they set out the plan.

'Tonight we are going to have dinner at 7.45 p.m., we're having a team meeting at 9 p.m., we'll be asleep at

10 p.m., up at 6 a.m. and at the show for 7 a.m.,' they explained.

Americans have a completely different work ethic to the British. Work hard, drink some coffee, go to bed. That was their mantra. I, on the other hand, was on tour in Germany. I wanted a German beer, I wanted a schnitzel. That was my mantra.

Dinner was a working dinner to talk about sales techniques and product spec. They ordered water, and I ordered a lager. As we talked and ate, I ordered another, then another. Those pilsners were going down a dream.

After about an hour one of them made a comment.

'Man, that's your third beer. Are you drunk?'

I laughed.

'Not yet mate.'

I could see the look of concern in his eyes and although I was fine, I eased back, just to stop him getting anxious because they'd obviously made a big investment in the exhibition, and I didn't want him thinking I was some loose cannon who was going to mess it all up for them.

The next morning, we started bright and early on our stall and after a slow first hour more people started coming in. It was mid-morning when this Italian geezer came over. He spoke English and I started talking to him. What's your name, where are you from, what are you interested in; that sort of chat. He told me that he had 30 bike shops around Italy. He was quite young and good-looking and he looked like the guvnor in a sharp suit. He had a beautiful assistant with him. He knew about the brand, and he liked it. We had a bit of a joke about Italian football and got on well. It turned out he had a big shopping list, and we had a lot of what he wanted. Over the next half hour or so, we went through the catalogue and when we finished, I'd sold him around £1 million worth of stock. It was my first day. I wasn't on commission, which in hindsight was a shame, but equally I'd been lucky. It wasn't a hard sale.

I brought one of the owners over to sign everything off and he could hardly contain his excitement. It turns out it was the biggest single deal his company had ever done. Both the partners were blown away.

'Teach me how to do that,' they said, after everything was finalised.

'Just make people like you, have a laugh. I was taking the Mickey out of Italian football and saying how good Italian cars are,' I explained.

After that the Americans loosened up and later in the afternoon one of them came back to the stand with several bottles of Grey Goose vodka, which we knocked back.

When the exhibition finished on the first day we all went to the high-end bar in the centre to carry on the celebrations. By that stage, with a £1 million deal sewn up, the Americans were in the mood to let off steam. We walked in and the Italian fella was in there with what looked like his family, including two distinguished looking older men. They called me over and I sat with them. I was quite pissed by that point and when the customer made me kiss one of the older man's hands and give the other one a kiss on each cheek, I just thought it was a friendly Continental thing to do.

We had a laugh and joke and I carried on gently taking the piss out of Italian football. Everyone was drinking and it turned into a party. At one stage I remember holding two shot glasses up to my eyeballs to impersonate one of the older men who was wearing glasses. I taught them how to say 'bosh'. We were having a great time.

'Bosh!' they were shouting.

'Boshetti!' I was shouting back.

The booze was flowing. It all got a bit hazy, but at some point in the evening someone came over to the table, tapped me on the shoulder and asked me to pop outside with him for a cigarette.

When we were safely away from prying ears he leaned in and said, 'You do know they're mafia, right?'

He was deadly serious and explained that the mafia owned a lot of cycle shops in Italy. They used them to launder money. I made a mental note to ease up on the banter. Luckily the older gentlemen – the dons – couldn't speak English.

Then I laughed.

'I made them an offer they couldn't refuse,' I replied.

# SKINNER'S SCRIPTURES

- People buy people, not products.

- A smile goes a long way.

- You catch more flies with honey than you do with vinegar.

- You win some, you lose some, but don't give up.

## CHAPTER 6

# EVERYONE MAKES MISTAKES

*'We need the Old Bill ... but we don't need them around us.'*

I've got a confession to make. I haven't always been a pillar of the community. You might have worked that out from some of the things I've already told you. So, while my mates at school were swapping Yu-Gi-Oh! cards in the playground, I was doing deals on DVD porn bundles. I wasn't a choir boy, let's put it that way.

When I was much younger, I got into a few scrapes and got in trouble with the law. I've changed now. I've got a family and responsibilities. Back then I had nothing to lose, so to be honest, getting caught doing something a little bit hooky didn't scare me too much. While I might have sailed close to the wind sometimes, one thing I never did was hurt anyone. When I did get involved in something a little bit dodgy I did it with good intentions, to give punters a bargain. I was like Robin Hood in that respect, a loveable rogue who didn't hurt anyone but could get you a cheap handbag that looked similar to a much more expensive one. Let's just say that I was on a quest to provide value for my customers. I've always liked helping people and nowadays I get loads of opportunities to give back, which I always do, be that supporting charities and causes or making donations.

Years ago I didn't have the platform I have now, so I found other ways of spreading a little happiness and lightening the load for people.

It started when I was just a teenager. It was soon after I'd been kicked out of school, so I was only about 14 or 15. I went to work for my dad initially. At the time, he had a warehouse in Rainham and he used to put DVDs into sweet shops. That was one of his businesses. They were legit movies, not porn, although knowing him, he probably did some under the counter deals as well. In those days, most convenience stores and newsagents had DVD racks in them and Dad stocked them. He went round collecting money for the DVDs that had been sold and restocked the racks with new ones. He kept the stock in his warehouse and my first job was rubbing stickers off the new DVDs that came in with white spirit and putting new price stickers on them, ready to go out on sale. I did that for about four days and realised it wasn't for me. After that I picked up a few days here and there on market stalls and one day ended up getting a few weeks' work for a company that sold advertising space. It wasn't my thing and I didn't tell them how young I was, but they liked me there and the geezer who owned the company could see that I was good at selling, so he took me to this sales conference where there were sales training events and workshops. That's where I met Joe.

Joe was a crook. Everyone else there was smart and driven and focused on being the best they could be. Joe looked right out of place. He was scruffy, shifty and rat-like, thin and a bit creepy. He stuck out like a sore thumb.

He must have recognised something in me because he sidled up to me and he said, 'There's something about you. You are a chap. You walk the walk and talk the talk. You've got potential.'

He was like that bloke Fagin from *Oliver Twist* who leads all the kids astray. I thought he was a weirdo, maybe a nonce, and asked him what he was after.

'The question you should ask is what do *you* want,' he said, all mysteriously. 'You're here because you want to make money and I've got something that will make you lots of money.'

I won't lie. That got my attention.

He then pulled out a plastic key from the inside pocket of his jacket and waved it in my face like a magician.

'This key puts £50 of electricity on anyone's pre-pay meter,' he said. 'All you have to do is push it in the slot and they get a £50 top-up.'

'Really?' I said.

'Straight up,' he nodded. He said it was spare promotional material from a utilities firm that the company salespeople used when they signed up new customers. I was only a kid, it sounded feasible to me.

'It's £2,000,' he said. 'Just for today, special price.'

I had savings from my DVD sales and I could see the potential in Joe's magic key so I took the plunge and agreed to buy it. After the conference, I went and got the readies and met Joe to hand over the money.

The next day I called a mate and explained that I was the proud owner of a magic electricity key that could do no end of good for the hard-up folk of Romford. I had a plan. I went out and bought a couple of hi-vis jackets and got them printed with a logo for a made-up company. I think it was Romford Utility Services. I then got a load of questionnaires printed up with about ten questions on them, all to do with electricity, how many times do you use a kettle a day, do you have gas or electric heating, that sort of thing.

There was a big council estate in Romford where 99 per cent of the homes were on top-up meters so that was the target. Me and my mate put on our hi-vis jackets, got a clipboard each, loaded up with questionnaires and went door knocking.

Previously, I'd tried the key out on a couple of mates and knew it worked but that first door was still a bit nervy, just in case it set off some kind of alarm. Our pitch was simple. We were from an electricity company doing a survey and if the homeowner agreed to answer our questionnaire, we had been authorised to offer them the one-time promotional offer of £50 of electricity for just £10. We could only accept cash.

I couldn't really see what was so wrong. Electricity is just there, right? It comes out of clouds in thunderstorms. We were giving people something that comes free in a lightning bolt. They benefited. We benefited. Everyone was happy.

So, we got to the front door and a woman answered. She was about 25 and I could hear a baby screaming in the background. I don't want to be unkind but it was obvious from where she was living that she was hard up.

'Good morning love,' I grinned. 'This is your lucky day.'

'Ere we go,' she said, rolling her eyes. She'd heard it all before.

'No, honestly, you're gonna love what we've got for you today.'

I launched into the patter about this once in a lifetime opportunity. I could see her eyes light up.

'How do I know it's not a load of bollocks,' she asked.

'Tell you what, I'll come in, put the money in the meter and if you believe it then, fill out the questionnaire and give us the money after.'

She agreed and me and my mate went in, slotted the key in her meter and hey-presto, her £2.10 credit turned into £52.10. She was over the moon and couldn't get the tenner out of her purse fast enough.

'Tell you what love,' I said, taking her money, 'don't even worry about the questionnaire, I'll fill it in for you.'

We spent the rest of the day knocking on doors and every single person said yes. It was easy. We plugged it in and boom! They had free leccy. Some people asked if they could have it twice.

'We're not meant to,' I'd say with a wink, 'but go on then, don't tell anyone.' They got £100 of electricity for a score.

We knocked on about a hundred doors that first day and then went back again the next day. Word spread and people would come up to us and ask us to come to their flat next. We covered the whole estate and people started asking if we'd come back and see them in a few weeks. It became a lucrative venture, and everyone loved us. We were the electricity fairies, sprinkling a little bit of magic in the homes of hard-pressed people.

Then one day we knocked on a door and gave our usual spiel and the elderly bloke who opened the door told us he couldn't speak to us.

'I had a letter from the energy company. I'm not allowed to accept any offers,' he said regretfully.

It was the same story with the next door we knocked. We realised that the game was up and our scheme providing cheap energy to the good people of Romford was over. It had been a nice little earner while it lasted.

I was young then and thought I was doing everyone a favour, and Joe's story about where he got his magic key from seemed believable to me at the time. And that's the thing about being a trader and a wheeler and dealer. You hear all the stories about where items have come from and why someone happens to have a pallet load of high-end cosmetics for sale at a knock-down price. Sometimes it's genuine, sometimes maybe not. In my younger days I trusted everyone. The world, it seemed, was full of lucky chances. I've heard them all.

'They delivered an extra pallet, and they couldn't send a lorry to collect it so they told us to keep it.'

'The wholesaler over-ordered by mistake and had to get rid of it.'

'Warehouse fire, mate. They had nowhere to store it so it's going cheap.'

'It's liquidated stock.'

'It's end-of-line.'

'They put the wrong labels on it, so it all has to go.'

And my personal favourite. 'They made it with the wrong type of cotton, and they can't sell it in their shops.'

In the trade, there are lots of reasons people give for why they have gear for sale. Some are more imaginative than others. Some are true, others, who knows? No one asks too many questions and there's a lot of trust. You get genuine bargains for a range of reasons. Some traders I know have deals with the big brands to take their seconds and end-of-lines. Some have contracts to rebrand the products to sell to the bargain stores. The high-end retailers and the big producers don't necessarily want to dilute the value of their brand by having their products turn up in Barry's Bargain Boutique, but they don't want to throw perfectly good stuff away if they can sell it somewhere, so they do deals with traders and wholesalers. If the customer gets a deal, everyone's happy.

Let's face it, everyone's out to nick a quid and the big companies are all pushing their luck and chancing it. I mean, look at Aldi and Cuthbert the Caterpillar. For those who don't remember, Aldi made a caterpillar-shaped cake and called it Cuthbert. It's fair to say that he bore more than a passing resemblance to Colin the Caterpillar, who is one of M&S's best-selling cakes. M&S were none too pleased and took Aldi to court to protect Colin from Cuthbert who was cheaper and who had no doubt been posing as Colin at kids' parties. It was hard to tell them apart. The supermarkets managed to come to an agreement and Cuthbert survived. Personally, I thought it was genius.

Poor old M&S seem to be in line for a lot of cheeky knockoffs. Their lawyers went to battle with sweet firm Swizzels arguing that their Pig Mug sweets looked just like Percy Pig, who is the geezer when it comes to chewy sweets. Lidl was accused of copying Percy too, but at least their Henry Hippo was a different species. They do say that imitation is the best form of flattery.

I mention these examples because they're just bigger scale versions of what a lot of clever traders do. You see products on bargain store shelves and on market stalls up and down the country that look familiar. They're just doing what the big boys do.

I cottoned on to this years ago when I introduced my own line of sparkling wine. I got the idea when I was in a posh store looking at their champagne range and realised that most of the labels looked the same and they were all the same shaped bottles. I took some pictures on my phone and put it to the back of my mind.

A while later I was out with Lanks delivering some stock and I saw a billboard advertising a wine warehouse in France.

'I really want to go wine tasting in France,' I said to Lanks.

And then I remembered my trip to the store. I had a mate who owned a printing firm that did labels so I went to him, showed him the labels I had and said, can you do something similar. He designed a label that looked the bollocks. I can't remember what we called it, probably something like Pom Derignon, or Choet et Mandon.

A week later, Lanks and I were in the car on the Eurotunnel on our way to stock up on vino. As usual, I didn't have a plan. I just figured we'd get to Calais, drive around a bit, and find somewhere. As it happens the plan worked perfectly because there were booze wholesalers all over the place in that part of France, catering for Brits on day trips looking for cheap plonk. I had cash, a bottle of posh champagne that I'd bought in the UK and a plan.

We found a wholesaler with a big warehouse, and I went up to the cashier.

'Excusez-moi,' I said, 'Do you speak English?'

'Of course I do,' she replied in a British accent. 'Everyone does.'

I showed her the champagne I had brought with me and asked if she had any bubbly in a similar bottle.

She looked at it for a second, thought, and then said they did stock something in the same shape and colour bottle, but it was sparkling wine, not champagne.

'How much is it?' I asked.

'Two euros,' she said.

At the time that was about £1.20.

She pointed me to an aisle, and I went to have a look. Sure enough the bottles were almost identical. I went back to the till and asked how many cases they had in stock. I bought as many as I could get in the car. We then had a look around, bought a few different beers and other bottles, had lunch and headed back home.

Operation Bosh Bubbly started the next day when I bought a label steamer and took the bottles to my nan's house.

Nanny Skinner was a legend. She was lovely but not a soft touch. She believed in tough love. She was covered in gold and got her first tattoo when she was 70. It was a rose. They used to call her the hardest woman in Harold Hill (that's where she lived). She didn't suffer fools, but she loved her family. Both my nans were lovely. My nan on my mother's side was more of a traditional, loving nan who cooked and fussed over you. They both got to see me on *The Apprentice* but sadly both died not long afterwards.

Nanny Skinner helped with my bubbly scheme, and we spent a day soaking and cleaning the cheap wine bottles in her bath, then steaming off the labels and applying the posh ones I'd had printed. Once rebranded the bottles looked premium.

I then took them round to corner shops and restaurants and sold them for a fraction of what they looked like they were worth. I sold them cheap, but the margins still made it worth the trip and the reports I had back from customers were all positive. One restaurant owner said it was better than the branded champagne he was selling. It was so popular that I got a regular little supply run going and returned to France several times to get stock.

I can't claim to be a saint. I've sold so much stuff over the years and that might have included a snide handbag here and there, or a fake Louis Vuitton belt. It's a hazard of the job and when I was younger and quite naïve, maybe I didn't ask as many questions as I would now. Some of the people I dealt with were unlikely to stick around if I started getting too curious about the source of the stuff they were flogging. 'What are you, Old Bill?' they'd say. Others just turned up randomly with a parcel, asked for cash and you never saw them again.

All this is why, when I was younger, I got nicked and convicted because I bought a parcel that turned out to be stolen. The Old Bill must have been watching me because I had the stuff in the back of the van and was driving to work when I pulled into a turning and was faced with a road-block. I pulled up and looked in the rearview mirror to see a cop throw a stinger out behind the van so I couldn't reverse. I got out of the cab and was promptly arrested. To be honest I think it was a bit dramatic for a few tubes of Body Shop cleansing gel, but I suppose they didn't know if I was a proper crook or not.

I was put on the floor and cuffed and told that all the stuff in the van was nicked. I explained that I genuinely didn't know and had bought it in good faith from some random geezer. I had no way of checking if the stock was stolen and paid the consequences for the mistake I made.

The upshot of it all was 300 hours community service, a fine and a two-year suspended sentence. That is now well in my past and I am a changed man.

I'm not surprised I got in scrapes when I was younger. Like I said before, I was naughty when I was a kid and have never been one for sticking to the rules. And I was surrounded by people who had a take-it-or-leave-it relation- ship with the law. One of the bits of advice I always remember Dad giving me was, 'Son, don't get tattoos because if you have tattoos they've got something to iden- tify you by.' By 'they' I assumed he meant *Crimewatch* viewers.

Now I know that this book is supposed to be motiva- tional and inspiring, as well as a bit of a laugh, and I'm absolutely not recommending that anyone breaks the law or gets into trouble. The point is, we all make mistakes, and we all deserve second chances and even if you have been a naughty boy or girl in the past, don't let that define you. People can change. Sometimes you do things because you feel you have to, or you feel pressured to do them. Be your own person and be proud of who you are. The big lesson in all this is that things don't come for free, no matter how much you duck or dive. Everyone gets caught in the end and the only real way to make something of yourself is to work hard.

The funny thing about all this is that I'm a great believer in law and order. I was shit scared of the police when I was a kid because they'd grab you and give you a smack if you misbehaved. They all seemed to be big, hard ex-military types around my way. Once me and my mates accidentally smashed a shop window when we were little while throwing stones at each other. The Old Bill were there in seconds and beat the fuck out of us. They even ran over my mate's push-bike in their squad car to teach him a lesson. It worked. We didn't do it again. You used to have to be 6 ft tall and a bit of a nutter to be Old Bill. Nowadays they're all tubby and look like they can't run more than 100 metres, which I know is an exaggeration, but I see some officers and think what kid is going to be scared of you.

I'm not dissing the police though. They do a hard job and an important job, and we should all support them. As some of my dodgier acquaintances would say, we need the police, but we don't need them around us.

# SKINNER'S SCRIPTURES

- Don't let your mistakes define you.

- If something seems to good to be true, sometimes it is.

- There's no short cut to success, hard work pays.

- If someone from Romford Utilities offers you free electric, be cautious.

## CHAPTER 7

# DON'T LOOK A GIFT HORSE IN THE MOUTH

*'You know me, I don't look*
*when I pour.'*

'BLIND-POURING' HAS BECOME a bit of a thing in my videos but people don't always understand what it means. It is the habit of never looking when you pour. It works for gravy, custard, Tabasco (caution advised) and brown sauce. Ketchup is a bit trickier because it doesn't easily pour, unless you have the stuff that's been watered down with vinegar and put in one of those plastic tomato-shaped squeezy bottles, in which case, squeeze away. For normal ketchup you need eye-on-bottle and two hands. Blind-pouring ketchup could take all day, and we haven't got time to waste.

The 'blind-pour' is a sign-off, but it's not just a gimmick. There's a message. What does it mean? Not looking when you pour is what real geezers do. It's a way of life: it means being fearless, having a healthy disregard for the rules (not the law, always follow the law!) and making the most of any opportunity that comes your way. Not looking when you pour is a metaphor for life. It is taking risks and not getting too upset when you fail or when you overcook the hot chilli sauce and your lips go numb.

Not looking when you pour is how I became the bedding king of Essex. An opportunity arose and I took it.

Here is what happened. I was sweeping out my warehouse which was on an industrial estate in Canvey Island. I had not long had my run-in with the law and rehabilitation and was back on my feet but still a long way from where I had been. The warehouse was full of bits and pieces, but nothing of great value. As I was replacing some boxes of stock on the racking that ran down either side of the building, I looked out the silver roll-up front shutter and saw a lorry drive past slowly. It was a small 3.5 tonne one with a covered back, old and belching out fumes. It went a few yards past my unit and stopped. The engine rattled when it was switched off and I heard the door open and shut. Ten seconds later a large bloke walked into the warehouse. He was about 20 stone and wore a grubby t-shirt that was too small for him, so his belly hung out the bottom. He had a big bald patch in the middle of his bonce which he had tried to cover with a greasy comb-over. He looked comical.

He opened his mouth, said hello and asked if this was my warehouse in an almost impenetrable Irish accent. He was a traveller.

'Sorry mate,' I pre-empted, 'I haven't got any scrap metal.'

He laughed and assured me that he wasn't after any old iron.

'I'm round the corner delivering to a big hotel, but they can't take in the mattresses I've got on board today and I have to get rid of them. I've got 30 and I'm almost giving them away. You can have them for £100 each,' he said.

My first thought was *fuck me, that's cheap*, but I'd never sold any before so didn't have a clue what they were worth. I told the bloke, who I later learned was called Rodney, that I wanted to check out what I might get for them first before I agreed to take them.

This happened in the days before smartphones (I had a Nokia) and I didn't have access to a computer so I rang one of my mates who worked in an office and asked him to have a look on the internet and see how much a standard double mattress was. They were dearer back then than they are now, and he tapped away on his keyboard and told me that they averaged between £500 and £600.

I looked at Rodney with my poker face and calmly said, 'Go on then, I'll have them.' Inside I was thinking, *result*!

He backed his lorry up and we unloaded them into the warehouse. Rodney gave me his number and explained that if I wanted any more, I should give him a call.

'Get a lot of cancelled orders, do you?' I asked.

'You'd be surprised,' he replied.

That afternoon I made a few calls and let some of my acquaintances know I had some mattresses for sale. I'd sold them all by the end of the day and made a decent profit. I'd taken the risk and gone with my gut. I had no idea whether there was a market for mattresses or not, but they were cheap and it was a random opportunity that paid off.

A few days later I called Rodney again and as luck would have it, he had some more mattresses that I bought from him and found homes for. Over the following months it turned out he had a lot of cancelled orders. We did quite a bit of business together and became good friends. He taught me about the bedding trade and introduced me to retailers and wholesalers. I became known as the go-to mattress guy. Then one day Rodney just disappeared. His phone rang off and I never saw him again. I have no idea what happened to him. He might have moved on, he might have gone on an all-inclusive break to one of His Majesty's hotels. He might have died. He might have retired and is currently sitting in a bungalow in Southend-on-Sea with his feet up watching *This Morning*. Who knows.

Rodney's disappearance put me in a tricky situation because by that time I was getting regular orders. I had to think quickly. I knew some wholesalers but none of them were offering the kind of prices Rodney was offering so I did another business 'blind-pour' and used a wholesaler in London for some orders but also decided to go directly to a manufacturer. That's when the idea for the bedding business really started to develop. Having learned about the sector I knew there were big mark-ups to be had. Mattresses are what businesspeople call a hero product. Everyone needs one, they don't break and very few get returned, unless a spring comes out. Each unit can net you up to £150 if you're not greedy so you only have to sell a handful a day to have a good day.

While I was selling wholesale stock, I started to investigate developing my own range. I brought five of the highest priced mattresses on the market, I took them to a manufacturer I found in Yorkshire and we cut them open, looked inside at how they were made and I asked the factory how much it would cost to make an equivalent product from scratch. Bearing in mind the test mattresses retailed at between £2,000 and £4,000, the manufacturer said they could make the same spec for about £200. My gob dropped open. I knew the big companies tucked up punters. That's what they all do, but these big brands were taking your trousers down. They still are.

Now, I know they argue that they have massive overheads, what with their logistics and marketing and staff costs and rents and all the rest. I understand that all too well, given what happened to me, but selling a £200 mattress for £4,000 seems like a proper liberty to me.

It gets worse when you get to the real high-end stuff because there's only so far you can go with a mattress in terms of quality. There are only so many springs you can physically put in them. Once you have a certain level of fabric you can't get any better. So generally, a £3,000 mattress is no different to one you pay £600 or £700 for. All you get for your extra £2,300 is a flash badge.

When I realised all this, I started offering people good mattresses at a decent price. I was still making money, but I was selling at £150 a mattress rather than £600. I started to do very well because people don't begrudge you making a profit as long as it's fair. Like I said before, everyone has to eat but some greedy fuckers want much bigger portions.

Another thing that I used to my advantage was that all the big firms don't hold stock. They take your money up front and then you join a queue and wait for them to make your mattress in around six to eight weeks (if you find yourself in this position, give me a shout).

I physically held stock so if you rang me up and said, 'Tom, I need a super king mattress and I have £600,' I'd say, 'I've got one here in stock, £650, same spec as a £4,000 one, made by me with a guarantee. You live in Glasgow? We'll have it to you by Thursday.'

How did we do it? We were hungry. I got a team around me, all friends, and we just got the job done and had fun doing it. It helped that I wasn't greedy.

What can I say? I like getting people a deal. It stems from my attitude back in the day on the markets when I sold clothes and would regularly tell punters not to go and pay £90 for a t-shirt when they could buy one made to the same pattern with the same material for a score from me.

The business was doing well and got even busier after *The Apprentice*. Being on the show didn't necessarily make life easier because although orders increased, I still had to do the work to fulfil them.

Then things really started to go mad during the pandemic when shops were shut, and people went mad ordering online. We were making deliveries all over the country and I started to use Twitter to tell people where we were and what we were doing. I was upbeat and positive.

'Remember lovely people, tough times don't last, tough people do.'

That was one of my regular messages because there was a lot of fear and uncertainty around and people needed to know that it would be alright. I never really looked at the messages and comments because as a dyslexic, I'm not great at concentrating on lots of words. But I could see people liked what I was doing. I think people just wanted to see that normal life was happening, that there was life out there, on the empty roads. Up until that point I'd only ever messed around with social media, but I had 100,000 followers thanks to being on the telly. I never really got involved in it for advertising and paying for clicks and all that stuff. I didn't understand it all. I just made videos, posted them and carried on working.

The orders kept coming in. People were moving in with each other. Kids were moving back home. Others were moving in with friends or elderly relatives, forming their bubbles and so lots of people needed beds. Later, as things started to settle down and everyone realised the world was not going to end, businesses started using the time and the government loans to invest and refit. Hotels ordered new beds and mattresses. Meanwhile people still had nowhere to spend money and many of those on furlough discovered they were better off because they didn't have the expenses of getting to work but were on the same money with nowhere to spend it. We drove around the country every day and there wasn't a day we didn't do less than 20 deliveries, which was easy because there was no traffic on the roads.

During lockdown it was the grafters who were out there and they were 'aving it, as they say. It was a great leveller. All the people who are overlooked in normal times – the delivery workers, the nurses, the supermarket workers – were suddenly recognised for the work they do. Normal working people who go out there and do a hard day's graft for an honest wage are the unsung heroes of the world. They get on and do their job, they are rarely thanked or appreciated. Often, they get tucked up by the big firms with crap wages and conditions and treated as disposable commodities that can be easily discarded or replaced. During lockdown they had their moment, and it was good to see. They were out there doing what they do, not complaining, working hard, and keeping the country going. I was proud to be out working too.

I did well and earned a decent amount of money. There were no pubs or restaurants open for me to spend it in, so for the first time in my life I managed to hold on to some of the money I was making.

Lanks and I were working six days a week because while the opportunity was there I wanted to make the most of it. Some people enjoyed sitting at home getting their furlough money but that wasn't for me. I could have taken a business loan and stayed at home baking and doing Joe Wicks work-outs, and there was nothing wrong with that. But Covid was another blind-pour moment in my life.

After lockdown the business continued to do well. I took on staff, opened retail units and grew. I did it all with no advertising budget. People ask me what the secret is, but to be honest I still don't know. I think it was because we offered affordable beds that got delivered quickly. The service was always good. The driver would take your bed to your room, and we'd ring you up a couple of weeks later to make sure everything was okay and asked happy customers to recommend us to their friends so we grew by word of mouth. In that respect there is no great secret to building a successful business based on sales. Be decent to people, be honest and don't rip them off. That's a rule for life too.

When we got big, work became my life. I was in the ware-house every morning loading up our vans before breakfast, then going back to the warehouse and the office. During the days I was in meetings and they started to drive me mad. I hate meetings. I'd be sitting there frustrated, listening to people talk bollocks about how they could improve the business, or why I should put money in their investment portfolios, while all I wanted to do was get in a van and get out on the road. I was seeing less and less of my son Henry, who was just a baby at the time. When it did all end, I was sad because I'd built it up from nothing, but I could also see it was a mixed blessing because it had become this monster that was draining all my time and energy. I was down, but I wasn't out, and I wasn't worried because I knew I could build back. I'd done it plenty of times before. I'm the comeback king. I'll have a go at anything, which is an advantage and a disadvantage because sometimes the things I try don't work out. If you don't take the risks, you don't get the gains.

After the bed business closed (and I'll explain why a little later), it took me about three or four months of graft working on the market stall every day to get back to a position where I could pay the bills. I worked with Collins and we worked hard, putting in 14-hour days, getting up at 4 a.m. going to the market and wholesaling gear on the phone.

Later, I got lucky with social media and TV work started coming in. That was all a fluke because the videos started to get noticed. Like I said before, I'm not a planner. I make things happen but I haven't got a strategy. Some might say I've been lucky, and luck plays a part, but you make your own luck in life.

I'm still out there grafting because it's in my blood. I still do the markets because I couldn't ever imagine not doing them. Without sounding like a knob I don't do it to earn, I do it because I love it. I go to the yard, I buy some stock, I go to Dino's and I've started expanding again with the boxing gym and Bosh workwear.

People say that they're surprised when they realise that I am who I say I am. I do go out and graft. I've still got the same mates I've always had and I'll still look after them. I have two lives. I have the one where I get to go on TV or radio, and then I have the normal life, where I'm eating my sunshine chicken curry at 5 a.m. in Dino's with Col the Cabbie and Collins.

I come from a place where nothing is guaranteed, and nothing is handed to you on a plate. You work through the hard times and celebrate the good times. There is no such thing as problems in my life, there are only solutions.

What's the lesson in all this? What can I tell you that might help you in your life? Firstly, accept that life isn't always going to run smoothly. You are going to have bad times, sometimes it'll be your fault that things go tits up, sometimes it will be beyond your control, but when it happens accept it and take responsibility for yourself. Put on your armour and get through it. Start from anywhere. Who says you have to start from page one? In life we are told to go to school, go to college, get a trade, work nine to five. That's not for everyone. I never did any of that, neither did most of the people I know, and we've all done okay, so do what works for you.

Start from the viewpoint that you're never going to get anything given to you, that you have to go out and earn it. Understand that if you want something in life, you have to go out and get it. If you put in the effort, you get the rewards eventually. I've had the beautiful cars and the best nights out, I have great friends around me and I have all that from hard graft. I've never had the luxury of asking a wealthy friend or family member for a handout. I'm not sure I would want one if it was offered. I've never been handed a job. I've never had an opportunity that I haven't found myself or put myself in a position for. Don't look to others to sort out your life for you. If you get help along the way, good for you, and if you need it, if you are struggling, then ask, but as much as you can, sort your own life out. It'll make you stronger, tougher and more resilient.

If you nick a few quid, celebrate it but don't go silly. Try and be a bit more sensible with your money than I was and am.

Always be friendly, always be polite and always smile. People buy from people they like. If you can walk into a room of strangers and walk out an hour later having made a positive impression, you've done well.

Be there for your friends and family because they'll be there when you need them. Be solid. Just be a decent human being and a bit of a geezer and see how far you get. Keep your feet on the ground, and remember, if I can do it anyone can.

# SKINNER'S SCRIPTURES

- Grab opportunities when they come your way.

- Say yes more than you say no.

- Make your own luck in life.

- Be the person who everyone remembers, for the right reasons.

## CHAPTER 8

# DOWN, BUT NEVER OUT

'Tough times don't last,
tough people do.'

I'M A MEDICAL miracle. You see, I've only got one kidney. I had a condition called reflux when I was very little. I won't go into medical detail about what reflux is because you don't really want to know about the ins and outs of my childhood waterworks, but basically it caused one kidney to wither away and die off.

I spent a lot of time in and out of hospital being checked and had to take medication for it for quite a few years. By rights I should have been a sickly child, but I don't ever remember it affecting me too much. When I was older the doctors told me I'd never be able to play sports and I'd never be able to drink alcohol. I proved them wrong on both points. It just goes to show that you shouldn't be defined by the problems you face in life; what counts is the way you overcome your problems and your challenges. Never give up, keep marching on because if you just keep going things will get better, whether it's in a couple of days, a week or a month.

Those of you who follow me on social media will know that I speak a lot about positivity, staying strong and overcoming hardships. Some people look at me and might wonder why I'm qualified to give out those messages. *He's been on the telly, he's got a few quid, he's doing alright.* But I can promise you that has not always been the case. There are still weeks when I have to find ways to cover bills and wages. I've been rich and poor and I have a terrible addiction to knocking out money. I can easily spend more in a week than I earn. That's always been my weak spot. I live by a simple philosophy: enjoy it while you've got it, make the most of every day and live for today. It sounds great, and it is, but it has also got me into trouble in the past. It all goes back to when I was younger and had zero responsibility. I could earn £1,000 on a Sunday on the market and once I'd packed up, counted my cash and got changed into my going out clobber, I'd be up the West End that evening like an idiot flashing the money and buying bottles of champagne. It was fun while it lasted but it never lasted long. Fast forward to Monday morning and I'd wake up skint with a hangover. The cycle started again. I'd drag myself out and head off to work hungry to make more money. In hindsight I was like a drug user, but instead of charlie, I had the jones for money.

There's no better motivation than being skint, but I understand now that there are two types of skint people. Those who think the world owes them a living and can't be

TOP LEFT: See – I've always been a smiler!

MIDDLE LEFT: Training for market-stall life.

Paying for new clothes inspired my early grafting.

After my school days were over earlier than planned, I set out grafting full time.

Come on, you lovely people!
Laughing monkeys –
two for a tenner.

One of my best mates, fellow
market-stall grafter Kimberley.

The ladies in
my life. Mum
and Sinéad.

Me and my fellow
Apprentices.

Ben Wilson aka Ben The Barber. Maybe not the best place to pose with a pint in hindsight!

Fancy a new pillow?

Dream car. Dream numberplate. Bosh! The two vehicles every grafter needs. A Bentley and a Transit.

How did I end up on *8 out of 10 Cats* with these legends?

Henry's birth. When Henry was born, this was what kept me going.

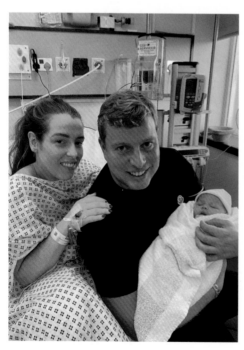

Welcome to the world,
Henry Skinner.

Friends and family
mean everything.

I'm just a bloke who sells stuff
out the back of a van.

Me and Big Lanks on the
night before my wedding.

Me and Sinéad on our
wedding day.

Henry and me in
Tenerife.

ABOVE: This is me in my natural environment, with Collins.

LEFT: Me at Bosh Gym with Brentwood's finest PT, Hughie.

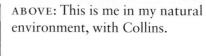

ABOVE: Ready to graft, after filling up at Dino's.

LEFT: Me and Kim with the legend that is my dad.

There's nothing better than having a few
friends round and cooking a meal.

Anton Ferdinand of the
West Ham Legends gives
the book his approval.

My epic team talk to West Ham before I leg it off
for the birth of the twins.

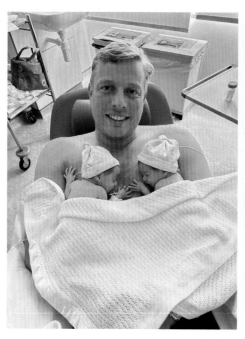

Me and the girls after my
dash back to the UK.

Henry meets his
little sisters.

My beautiful daughters.

bothered to get their heads down and graft, and those that take being skint as a challenge and a motivation to go out and work. Obviously, I'm simplifying here because there are people who for any number of reasons can't work, maybe through illness or family circumstances. They deserve help and compassion. But if you are skint and you can work, there are no excuses. Get off your arse and get out there. Stand proudly on your own two feet.

I didn't like having nothing. I still don't, and that makes me hungry. I used to hang around in places full of city brokers in suits earning mega-money bonuses and I tried to keep up, tried to be like them and kept pushing myself to work harder and longer and to find better deals.

I was in my early twenties and I was fed up with not having enough. The truth of the matter was that I did have plenty. I was doing well but I was spending it all. People around me would say 'Tom, you do really well' but I couldn't see it. As far as I was concerned, I was trying to live a champagne lifestyle on lemonade money.

I do remember thinking it was unsustainable, particularly because I eventually wanted a family and a nice house and my own business. I invested in property and had my own flat but even then, I sometimes struggled with the payments. Eventually, it all went wrong after I got arrested. I'd sunk all my money into the stock and when that was confiscated, I had nothing. It wasn't the first time. It happened before when my van got stolen, but this time I had more outgoings.

I couldn't afford my flat, my dad had moved away and I ended up back at my mum's having to start again from scratch. Some days I didn't even have a tenner to put fuel in the van. It was a hard lesson to learn. To be honest, it felt humiliating. I went from Tommy Big Bollocks, the champagne maestro of Mayfair, to some geezer down on his luck sleeping on a futon in his mum's lounge.

At the time, Mum lived in a two-bedroomed house. My brother lived there too so the only room left was the lounge. I went and bought the futon from Argos for £50 which I folded out each night. I was so embarrassed to be in that position that I waited until everyone had gone to bed before I rolled it out to sleep on and made sure I woke at 5 a.m. every morning to put it away so no one saw me. Mum was brilliant and said I could stay for as long as I wanted. She used to make me sandwiches for the morning to take to work so I didn't have to buy lunch. I am forever grateful to her, but I also knew I had to get out and stand on my own two feet financially again as soon as I could.

There was no quick fix and no miracle five-step programme to becoming a millionaire. Life ain't like that. In the words of the wise Irish philosopher Ronan Keating, 'Life is a roller coaster, just gotta ride it.' I knew the only way back from the futon on the floor was through work. No one was going to swoop in and give me a wad. Instead, I slogged through it. I went out every day, started small, nicked a quid here and a quid there, gradually built up my stock and most importantly stayed away from the temptations of Mayfair. Every now and then I treated myself to a Toby Carvery, if I'd had a good week. In the end, after several months and a bad back from the futon, I scraped together enough for a deposit on a small flat and moved out.

In today's world, it's easy to get hooked on the idea that you should have a life of luxury and that you can get what you want without having to work for it, that you can just whack it on a card because you deserve it. We're constantly bombarded with messages that tell us that we should be able to have the latest gadgets, the most expensive clothes, flash cars and luxury holidays. There's nothing wrong with enjoying any of these, but the thing you must remember is that these things don't come free. If you want something, you have to work for it, unless you are royalty, have a trust fund or win the lottery. For the rest of us, hard work is the only path to success.

You work hard, you learn and grow, you develop new skills, and become more confident. I couldn't be proud of myself if I didn't work and there is something fulfilling about doing a hard week's work, finishing on a Friday and having a pint. In my opinion, it's one of your key human rights.

Hard work builds character, resilience and determination. It makes you self-sufficient so you are not dependent on others, or your mum. It puts you in control of your own life.

That blip in my early twenties was not the only time I found myself going back to zero and starting from scratch. Throughout life I've found myself on top and back down. In life sometimes you win, sometimes you lose. You can't be at all the weddings and none of the funerals. You have to be at both. The lesson in all this is that when you are down, when things don't go right, learn from it. Any successful person you meet will tell you that not everything they touch turns to gold, but that doesn't stop them trying new things and taking risks. When they fail, they take the time to learn from their mistakes and figure out what they can do differently next time.

Failure can be a great teacher. It helps you realise your weaknesses and shows you where you can improve. For this reason, there's no point trying to blame other people or making excuses. Own your failures because then you can understand what went wrong and make sure it doesn't happen again.

Failure is tough, but it makes you tougher, more resilient and determined. When you fail, it is important to pick yourself up and keep going.

Some people will only talk about their successes and give you the impression their life has been one smooth journey up the ladder. That's not how life works. The road is bumpy but if you work hard, it's a gradual climb up.

Sometimes though, things happen that knock you backwards and that are beyond your control. Some of the reasons that my bedding company had to close a few years ago were down to decisions I made but other factors were far beyond my control.

The company grew quickly after I finished *The Apprentice* and did very well thanks to massive demand during the pandemic when everyone had money to spare and plenty of time to spend in bed.

By the early 2020s, I had a business taking in £130,000 a week and employed 14 staff. An investor offered to buy it for £1 million but I thought it was worth much more than that and turned them down. In my mind it was worth at least £5 million. I was like one of those deluded people who go on *Dragons' Den* and massively overvalue their business. I had plans to expand everywhere and pump the profits into new shops and retail spaces. Our flagship store was in Lakeside. I spent £100,000 fitting it out. I bought a chandelier for £5,000 for one of the shops. Why? Because I was an idiot. I needed to find £33,000 a week just to cover my overheads. That's a lot of mattresses.

But I was doing okay. I had mates around me helping me but a lot of others who thought I was a millionaire and a human ATM. I was helping people out, lending money that I never got back. Several people who I thought were my mates took money from me and then never even had the courtesy to explain why they didn't pay me back. I wouldn't have minded. It wasn't about the money. What really hurt was that they took advantage of me. It was an expensive lesson to learn, and I found out who my true mates were.

At the heart of my problem was the fact that I got a lot of financial success quickly and didn't understand it or know how to manage it. In hindsight, that's why it would have been good to have Lord Sugar as a partner as he would have been more sensible.

But the other element to the downfall was beyond even Lord Sugar's control. In February 2022, Russia invaded Ukraine and costs for everything doubled overnight, including the beds we sold. A divan base that cost me £65 and provided a nice margin went to £145 plus VAT. Electricity went up. Diesel went to £2.20 a litre, people started to struggle and then to top it all, Liz Truss tanked the economy with her loony mini-budget. Nice one Liz. Overnight my business went from making a few quid to not making any money and I still had all my overheads to cover. I'll be honest with you, it wasn't a fun time. I was shitting myself.

When I look back at the figures, I had such large over-heads that even when I was doing well and had millions in turnover the profits were small and we weren't making enough. I remember realising one day that I could make more money on a market stall without the huge pressures or responsibility. People think it's all Bentleys and golf clubs, but the reality was that I sold the Bentley long ago to raise money for the business and I didn't have time for golf because I was working seven days a week.

There's a saying that money attracts money. I'm not so sure. I think money is like water, the more you get, the quicker it flows away. For example, I had a meeting with a company of agents who promised to get me 4,000 sales, which was all great, but lunch came to £5,000, the company took £5,000 in commission so that's a chunk of the profits gone before you've even started. Then there are transportation costs, licensing costs, staff, the internet bill, the website bill, the electricity, the rent, the marketing and all the other things running a business is about, versus me and a mate, on a market stall, having a laugh. The harder it became to make a profit, the more I started to question whether I was being a mug for trying to keep it going. And in the end, I was putting several thousand a week of my own money in to keep it afloat. It was unsustainable. There was nothing left and I still had to find a way to pay the warehousing, manufacturers and staff.

I was gutted but I knew I had to close it. It was my baby. I had built it up from nothing with hard work and determination and it was hard to see it fail, particularly when the main factor for the failure was happening 1,500 miles away. Vladimir Putin, in my opinion, is a twat.

I sat down with my dad one day and asked him what he thought I should do.

'Mate,' he said, 'nothing lasts forever. You've been so unlucky, but you've just got to let it go.'

And that's what I did. I sold part of the business to

another company but never saw any money and the only thing I kept was a big Luton van and a warehouse full of stock, which amounted to odds and sods.

It's all learning, and it was probably the best thing that ever happened to me because money wasn't real after *The Apprentice*. I lost my respect for it because it was easy to earn.

When people ask me, I'm honest and I tell them I'm a crap businessman. My problem is I always get there and then I get carried away. I get mad ideas. I spend thousands developing a crazy product. My Kryptonite was wanting to be a big brand. I still do. Since *The Apprentice* I've started Bosh Gyms, Bosh Workwear, and there might be a Bosh beer in the future. I hope I've learned, and I don't mess it up again, but if I do, so be it. It's better to have a go and fail than be ruled by fear and never try.

If you stick at it, something always turns up. My team, West Ham, has a song, 'I'm Forever Blowing Bubbles'. If you ever go to a game you'll hear it ringing out from the stadium. Every fan knows it and it is one of the most fitting songs you could imagine for the type of people who come from the club's traditional heartland, the East End and Essex. One line particularly says it all. 'Fortune's always hiding.' It is sung the loudest. All the fans understand that fortune does hide, but if you keep looking, sometimes you find it.

After I closed the business, I decided to take a walk around Romford Market, where it all started. I was there with my tail between my legs and I spoke to my mate Ross. He's a social media expert. I'm not.

'You need to go back to basics,' he said. When we were delivering beds during lockdown I used to do little videos which I posted on Twitter telling people where we were and what we were up to. I always included a bit of banter in them, I was always upbeat because that's just who I am and I made sure they were positive because it was a tough time for a lot of people and they needed hope.

I never really paid much attention to the comments, but Ross did.

'You need to do more of that,' he said. 'You don't post enough on social media. Social media is where you can make some serious money. Get back to posting online.'

I looked around me and the market was full of life. There were people buying and people selling. There was opportunity. Fortune was hiding there in plain sight. There and then I decided I was going back on the markets to graft and build back up. I made a video walking around that market and posted it online and I've made one every day since, sharing my thoughts and giving people a bit of motivation. Then Dino's happened and the rest, as they say, is history.

So, what can I share with you about hitting rock bottom? The biggest lesson is that when you are at the bottom and things can't get any worse, that's the time to keep going because if they can't get any worse, they can only get better. Don't give up because you've done the hard part. You might as well keep going. Anything is possible, all you have to do is overcome fear and keep moving forward.

If you told me years ago when I was in debt and sleeping on a floor that I would have a stunning missus, a beautiful family, lovely cars, a busy business and fantastic friends, I would have laughed at you. But I worked hard and kept myself out of trouble. No one can take that away from me.

You might be afraid, and you might be anxious, but if you don't try you'll never know. And if you fail you are always going to get it wrong so you've not lost anything, you've just got the failure out of the way so next time you can succeed. Nine times out of ten when you try something new you will get it wrong, so you can either not do that thing and never succeed or you can do it, fail, learn and then get it right. You are going to make mistakes so you might as well make that mistake now, rather than be scared and make it anyway a few weeks or years later. The harder you work the luckier you get, and the luckier you get the more opportunities come your way.

# SKINNER'S SCRIPTURES

- Keep marching forward when you're at rock bottom, the only way is up.

- Hard work is the only way to success.

- If you want something, you need to work for it.

- You can't be at all the weddings and none of the funerals.

## CHAPTER 9
# THE KING OF ROMFORD

*'Motivating the nation one
breakfast at a time.'*

THE FUNNY THING about how my life has turned out is that I never fancied being famous. In my line of work, it usually pays not to have a particularly high profile. Flying under the radar was the rule of thumb. Not that I wasn't well-known in my manor. Long before I appeared on *The Apprentice* I earned myself the nickname 'King of Romford' because I was the man who could get you anything.

I'm not even sure I'm famous now. I suppose the fact that I'm writing a book means that I probably am. And I get recognised when I'm out and people want selfies with me, which is great. I always like to stop and chat to people. But what is it I actually do? What am I famous for? Fucked if I know! I'm a normal bloke from Romford who gets up early, goes out to work, eats mental breakfasts, likes a beer on a Friday and says 'bosh' a lot.

Like most things that have happened to me, it was fate. I didn't intentionally get famous. I never went seeking attention. I wasn't one of those people who grew up with a burning ambition to be a celebrity. I didn't watch *Love*

*Island* and think, that's a bit of me, that is. I didn't watch *Love Island* full stop. Canvey Island, maybe. But *Love Island*? Nah.

I'll let you into a secret. Before I went on *The Apprentice* (which I never wanted to go on) I turned down an opportunity to be a telly star. I could have been one of the cast of *TOWIE*. They wanted me to go on the show and for a laugh I even went to a meeting with the production company because one of my mates was in the running to go on it.

It was back when the programme first started, and my mate Lou was one of the people they were looking to get on the show. She knew Gemma Collins – now known as The GC – and Gemma did all her *TOWIE* interviews at Lou's house. Lou had been given a contract to sign and had even been to see Graham, the psychologist from *The Jeremy Kyle Show* who ITV was using to make sure the *TOWIE* candidates were mentally fit to cope with being on the show. Lou passed her psychological assessment with flying colours and was deemed mentally fit to mix up with Mark Wright and Bobby Norris and the rest of the mob. At the time the plan was for Lou and Gemma to start on the show together. Each cast member had an entourage of characters and associates that appeared on the show with them and me and my mate Kim, Lou's sister, were going to be included as part of Lou's extended family.

The production team asked me and Lou to go up to their offices in London for an interview. They wanted to see how we interacted together and to find out a bit more about me. I had no experience of anything like that at the time but know now that TV companies hold casting sessions for people in reality shows in the same way they hold casting sessions for actors. The people in these shows are carefully selected. Just because you live in Brentwood, have a big house and Turkey teeth and wear loafers without socks, doesn't automatically qualify you for a part in *TOWIE*. When *TOWIE* first came out, no one could understand what it was. Was it reality or was it some kind of soap? They called it 'scripted reality', which basically means the people in it are real and not actors but they are directed into certain situations and told what to say and how to react.

Anyway, enough about the secrets of TV. Lou and I decided we'd make a day out of our trip to the *TOWIE* offices. I was going through one of my skint periods at the time and had about £40 on me and some plastic and when I went to the cashpoint to get some more readies it told me I had £12 left in my account. I also had to dodge past the barber because I owed him £20 for a haircut. This was not an unusual set of circumstances. Life was often feast or famine. I remembered that I'd run out of aftershave and went into Boots on the way to use one of their testers, so I probably went into the interview stinking of Kouros. Lou, on the other hand, had just sold her house, so she had a bit of money. We got to Liverpool Street Station a few hours early so Lou suggested we find a bar and have a drink.

We found a place, sat down at a table and Lou asked, 'What do you want, Veuve?'

I hadn't told her I had no money but if she wanted champagne, I wasn't going to stop her. We ended up drinking two bottles and neither of us have any recollection of who paid the bill. She thought I did, and I thought she did. We were both too pissed to remember. It never appeared on any of my credit card bills so I assume she did.

Off we staggered to the *TOWIE* offices where we messed around with the production staff. After that we went to Palm Beach Casino in Mayfair where I threw my £40 on number six on the roulette table and it came in. Suddenly I was flush with £1,400. Bosh! We had a night out and got a black cab all the way home.

Despite being drunk I must have made an impression because I got a call a few days later telling me they wanted me on the show. I'd only gone up for a laugh and I declined their offer straight away. At the time my life involved selling gear from the back of a van, so I had no interest in being involved in the programme. And I couldn't see the *TOWIE* production team getting themselves down the market at 5 a.m. to film me anyway. For some reason Lou never got on the show either, but Gemma did. We could never work out why they pulled the plug, but in hindsight it was probably for the best.

*The Apprentice* was also a fluke. At the time I had my mattress company and had set up a pillow company too, selling pillows in markets. It was doing okay but I hadn't reached the next level. I didn't have the kind of money needed to get there. I didn't have an investor.

Sinéad is a massive fan of the programme. I knew about the show and had watched bits of it, but I can't sit still for that long, which is why I don't watch much telly. I knew who Lord Sugar was though and I respected him as a businessman, although I wasn't so sure about his choice of football team (he's a massive Tottenham fan). Sinéad on the other hand was obsessed by the series. I joked that she wore a tie to watch it. She would often pick the winner right at the start of the series.

Anyway, she was watching it one day and at the end of the show the advert for contestants for the next series came on.

'Do you think you have what it takes to be Lord Sugar's next business partner?' it read.

Sinéad turned to me and said, 'Tom, you need to apply. You'd be brilliant on it. Think how much it would help with the pillow business.'

'Babe,' I said, 'why would they want me? I'm some bloke who sells stuff out the back of a van. I've never worn a suit in my life.'

She was having none of it.

'I'm telling you, you'd be brilliant on it. You need to apply.'

I played the dyslexia card.

'I can't do forms,' I protested.

'I'll do it for you,' she said.

And that's what she did. She filled out the form for me and we stretched the truth a bit: avid churchgoer, never swears, has seven business degrees, that kind of stuff. Sinéad said it felt like filling out a lottery form. You can dream about winning but deep down you know it's very unlikely to happen. Apparently, that year about 40,000 people applied. We didn't hear anything for months and I'd completely forgotten about it. Then I got an email. I was as surprised as anyone when I read it and it said they loved the application form and could I go for a trial. I protested because the auditions were held on a Friday, which is beer time with the lads, but Sinéad told me to stop being an idiot and to go along.

'What have you got to lose?' she asked.

From my limited knowledge of the show, I remembered that all the blokes wore a suit, which was a problem for me because I'm not a smart dresser. I had one suit at the time, a funeral suit. I have two looks. In the summer it's Reebok classics, a pair of shorts and a Ralph Lauren polo shirt. In the winter it's a flat cap, a jacket, trousers and a pair of boots. I'm usually scruffy but I always make sure I have a nice pair of boots and a decent hat.

Realising that I was going to look out of place at the auditions, I went to Lakeside to buy a new polo shirt but got a long-sleeved one because it was a bit smarter. I put it on with jeans and my best Timberlands.

I was still adamant that I'd be found out straight away and wouldn't make it past the first level. *Why would they want me?*, I thought. I had a chequered past. I worked on market stalls. I was not really your Lord Sugar Apprentice candidate type. I'd never worked for a corporate company; I didn't go to college or university. I was thrown out of school.

But I'm also a big believer in saying yes when opportunity knocks, and if you don't give it a go, you never know. I went along and sure enough I walked into the big studio-type building, and it was full of people with three-piece suits on, carrying Filofaxes and briefcases (I might be exaggerating slightly). I stood out like a sore thumb but didn't feel intimidated in any way and approached it in the same way I approach most situations in life, as a bit of a laugh. I went in, made friends, had a joke, and took the piss out of people in a well-meaning way, joking that I'd never seen so many shit suits in one place before.

We were all on the ground floor of the building milling around in a big open space and there was a glass-fronted observation room above us. I could see people behind the glass looking down, clipboards in hands, making notes. It was like being in some kind of experiment. A few of them pointed at me occasionally and spoke to each other. I kept catching their eyes and waving.

We got put in groups and taken into another room and each given a number. Mine was 13, which is unlucky. I wasn't having that. Six is my lucky number so I found number six and swapped with him. We then had to say a bit ourselves and tell the clipboard people why we should be Lord Sugar's apprentice.

One after another the candidates gave their spiel.

'My name's John, I work in banking and I should be Lord Sugar's apprentice because I am very good with numbers.'

'My name's Darren. I've been to university. I've done this and that and I can sell anything.'

They called out for number six. I had 30 seconds.

I took a breath and went into full-on market trader mode.

'How are we doing today ladies and gentlemen? I must say, everyone is looking fantastic today. I hope you are having a lovely time. Now listen, the first thing I need to tell you is that my name's Tom Skinner. I'm a market trader from Romford, East London. I like to buy and sell and I'll nick Lord Sugar a couple of quid because I'm good at selling but pony at everything else.'

People laughed. They seemed to like me.

The next task I was set was to sell my own boot to one of the facilitators. *Easy*, I thought, *I'll use a little gimmick we use on the markets.*

I took off my boot and handed it to the person I was supposed to sell it to and asked her a question.

'How much do you reckon you would pay for that boot?'

She looked at the boot, frowned, thought for a second and then answered.

'About £50?' she said.

'Sold!' I said, clapping my hands to seal the deal.

Everyone laughed.

At the end of the tasks, they started calling numbers out and asked everyone whose number was called to stand to one side. Number six was called and I went to stand with the group, expecting that I'd be sent home. I genuinely assumed I was in the reject pile and was surprised when I heard: 'Congratulations. You've made it to the next level.'

I started to think that maybe I was in with a chance. Me and the remaining candidates were then sent upstairs where we were interviewed one-on-one. One of the questions was, 'why did you apply?' Most people took pains to point out that they didn't apply because they wanted to be on telly. No, they applied because they wanted to add value to Lord Sugar's business empire, and they believed they would make the perfect business partner. Bullshit!

'Course I want to be on telly, that's why I'm here, I wouldn't have come if I didn't,' I said.

The whole process was good fun. I didn't treat it seriously and as the day went on the field narrowed down. Other people disappeared until there were just a few dozen left. We were all told that we'd be contacted in the next few days with a decision. I still assumed that I wouldn't be in the final line-up. I'd obviously entertained them for the day, but I still believed that people like me didn't get on *The Apprentice*. Sinéad had a bit more faith when I told her I lasted the day and she reckoned I'd be picked.

Over the next few days, I told a few mates that I'd been to the auditions and inevitably the prank calls started.

'Hello, is that Mr Skinner? It's Barry from the BBC. You've got the job!'

No one fooled me.

'Fuck off!' I laughed and hung up.

About five days after the auditions my phone rang. It was a call from a withheld number.

'Is that Thomas Skinner?'

'Yes mate, who is this?'

'It's *The Apprentice*. We are delighted to say that you've been selected.'

'Will you please just fuck off!' I sighed and hung up.

A few seconds later the phone rang again. The same withheld number.

I answered.

'Mate, stop it now, it's getting boring!'

Then urgently before I hung up, 'No, wait. It really is the BBC. You are through to the show.'

And that's how it happened. It was a fluke, and I still didn't fully believe it until I went to have my photograph done for the publicity material. That was a joke too. I had to go out and buy a three-piece suit because they weren't going to stand for a polo shirt and jeans. The day before the shoot I was training in the gym and doing some sparring and got smacked in the face so by the time I turned up to the studio I had a big black eye which they had to photoshop out.

One of the rules about being on *The Apprentice* is that you can't tell anyone, except for your immediate family. Of course, I told a few of my mates who told their mates, but not one of them believed me.

I was then taken away for seven and a half weeks. They take your phone. You can't watch TV or read newspapers and every few weeks you get to call your family for a few minutes while someone from the production crew sits with you to make sure you don't give anything away. You are totally isolated. For one of the tasks, we were flown to South Africa for nine days and my family didn't even know I'd gone, there was no emergency number. It was like being kidnapped but much more fun.

I learned some trade secrets which made me laugh. The taxi bit at the end, when the contestant who's been fired explains how you've not seen the last of them because they're a winner, or variations on that theme, is filmed at the start of the show, before anyone's fired. And the boardroom is in a warehouse near White City, not at the top of a skyscraper in Canary Wharf. The tasks are also done over several days and the boardroom scenes are full of re-takes. It's not as seamless as it looks. It is all edited together. I didn't realise how much I say 'bosh' until I saw myself on it and I think they added a few in there to make it look like I had bosh Tourette's.

The first time I met Lord Sugar was in the boardroom. We all had to write a few words to describe ourselves. There were the ones you'd expect, like 'successful' and 'entrepreneur'. I wrote 'jammy' because I am. I could fall over in shit and get up smelling of roses.

One of the geezers called himself a falcon and Lord Sugar started taking the piss. I started laughing. Lord Sugar shot me a look and asked what I was laughing about.

'Because it's funny, you're ripping into him.'

Lord Sugar looked at his notes and said, 'You're Thomas? On here it says you're jammy, what are you a doughnut?'

'I probably am,' I replied. 'Do you like doughnuts? I bet you do.'

We got on alright, me and Lord Sugar. The contestants didn't have loads of interaction with him, but I did have a few chats and asked him what the football scores were because I wasn't allowed access to the outside world. When I was finally fired he said to me, 'Tom, you know what I notice about you? When people walk in and out the boardroom, you always open the door for everyone.' Like me, he is a man who respects and values good manners.

The other contestants were all alright. Some were on it to be famous but most of them were there because of business. They took it seriously and it does test your skills.

Living inside the house was how I imagined it would be on *Big Brother*. We were isolated from the outside world as much as we could be and there was always someone from the production crew with us. Everything was set up for the cameras. All the chats about who is or isn't going to be fired that week, the morning call from Lord Sugar. It's all staged.

I didn't mind it and just got on with people. I chatted to everyone. Some people formed good friendships and their own groups. A lot were trying to win and there was games-manship, as you might expect. Most days you worked on the tasks until the evening so we would just come back late, eat and go to bed. I did all the cooking in the house because I like cooking and I like having things to do. Otherwise I would have been bored. The strangest thing was sharing a room with two other blokes.

One of the highlights that people remember was when I took one of the contestant's place in the boardroom after the team leader had picked her to face the firing line. The team leader was a guy called Ryan-Mark. He was a bit of a character, and I liked him. The task was organising an away-day and we failed after one customer demanded a refund because we didn't supply a gluten-free option. Ryan-Mark chose two girls, Marianne and Pamela, to face Lord Sugar for the sack. I'd been on the sub-team with Pamela and she was really good. The task certainly didn't fail due to her, and she didn't deserve to take the flak. When Ryan-Mark picked her, I thought *hang on, she's good at business, she has a chance to go far in this, she shouldn't be going out.* I told Ryan-Mark, 'I don't think you should be bring-ing Pamela back at all.'

Lord Sugar butted in and asked if I'd like to take her place.

I agreed. 'I'm being serious because I won't have it. She should not be coming back in this room 100 per cent,' I said.

No one had put themselves in the firing line like that before on the show. Generally, by the time it got down to the three candidates for the chop it was every man and woman for themselves. Viewers love it when people start stabbing each other in the back. I didn't think Ryan-Mark had made a fair decision, so I took a stand. It was also a smart move because I figured it would be hard for Lord Sugar to fire me after I'd offered to nominate myself. And he didn't, he fired Ryan-Mark.

After I left the show, I didn't see the rest of the candidates very often. We all had our own lives to get back to, but we did have a group-chat.

I was involved for seven weeks and on the show I lasted nine out of the ten weeks it was broadcast and lost every task. I'm a survivor. I was probably good for viewing figures. The only task I didn't get to do were the interviews which I would have loved because I would have given it back to them when they started trying to bring me down, which is what they usually do.

I would have worked for Lord Sugar if I had won, but I wouldn't have done as well as I am now because under the terms of the contract, they take half your business away. So they do invest the money but you lose a massive chunk of your business.

I came out of the show at the end of May 2019 and the series wasn't broadcast until October, so until then I still wasn't really allowed to tell anyone I'd been on it, but in reality that's impossible. While I was away Big Lanks started a rumour down the pub that I had been nicked by trading standards for selling snide Ralph Lauren jumpers down the market and had been put in Chelmsford prison.

When I came out, me and the family went to the Isle of Wight with my mum for her birthday and then came back and had a BBQ. All my mates were there too, and it was like a welcome home party. I didn't know about Lanks' rumour.

One mate came over for a chat.

'Tommy, you're back. How was it in there?'

'It was alright, but I was gutted I couldn't ring any of you,' I said.

'It's alright mate, we've all been there, we know what it's like.'

How did he know what it was like on a reality TV show? Then he handed me a couple of hundred quid rolled up.

'What's that for?' I asked.

'You haven't been able to earn for a few weeks, it'll help you get back on your feet.'

*That's very generous*, I thought.

Then another mate came over.

'Here's a monkey for you until you get yourself straight,' he said, handing me another wad of notes. 'How did you get on in there?'

I was a bit confused but my mates are the type of mates who look after their own.

'It was alright, but the food was shit,' I said.

'It's shit in every one of them,' he nodded. I didn't twig until another mate said I was lucky I only got seven weeks.

'We all thought you'd get at least six months,' he said.

'It ain't on for six months, it only goes on for ten weeks.' Then the penny dropped.

'I wasn't inside, I was filming *The Apprentice*,' I told him.

'Pull the other one. It's nothing to be ashamed about. We've all been there,' he said, putting an arm around me and laughing.

Despite repeatedly explaining that I had been a contestant on *The Apprentice* to everyone who knew me over the following months, no one believed me. The general consensus was 'why the fuck would Tom Skinner be on *The Apprentice*?' Which was exactly what I thought when Sinéad said I should apply, so who could blame them?

When the line up for series 15 finally appeared in the newspaper and there was a big picture of me with my photoshopped face wearing a three-piece suit they couldn't believe it.

A lot changed afterwards. Things went mental and I got recognised everywhere. The first time it really hit home was when I was mobbed by kids shouting 'bosh' at me in Lakeside. They all wanted selfies. It helped the business too. It's not really stopped. I can still get people shouting 'bosh' out their motors at me. Even now, years later, people still tell me how much they enjoyed watching me on the show. I suppose I stood out a bit.

It might have all died down after a couple of years and I'd just be another forgotten reality TV contestant if it wasn't for the social media posts.

Like I've said before, I never had ambitions to be a social media influencer, I don't even know what that really means. I know there are loads of people who post fake photos and videos of cars they rent and places they go that they can't afford. They pretend they are living some sort of perfect life, but that kind of 'life through photoshop' has never been me, except for my *Apprentice* publicity shots, and that was filtered for a reason.

The social media profile happened by accident. After *The Apprentice* things got very busy with the bed and pillows companies and I carried on posting. Then during the pandemic, Lanks filmed me when we were out delivering, and my followers started to increase because the positivity and the messages I was giving really perked people up.

At first I didn't know they were having an impact but then mates started telling me about some of the comments people were leaving and I could see the number of followers increasing. There were comments such as 'I was feeling down today, I was going to stay in bed and not go to work, but you've given me the motivation to get up' and 'This made my day, I wake up every morning and wait to see what you post. It makes me feel better, it gets me started for the day'. I realised it was inspiring people to get up and go out and give it 110 per cent. I keep doing it because I figured if it was helping people then it was important. That's how it was built.

As far as I can see, a lot of people on Instagram make people miserable because they post stuff about their perfect lives and people look at it and think they can never measure up. My posts were just me in a van, or with a mug of tea and more recently in Dino's with a sunshine curry, or at home with a Cornetto. I was in places people could relate to, telling them that I understood that their lives were hard sometimes, but that they just had to push on through, work hard and do the best they could. I think people are tired of filters and stuff that isn't true. How can you relate to someone draped in Gucci who's in a different rooftop bar in Dubai every week?

The interest in my posts got even bigger after I started posting from Dino's. People liked the motivational messages, which all come from the heart and are never prepared or scripted – I just say what's on my mind that morning – and they also became fascinated with what I have for breakfast. I mean, some people get obsessed by it. There's a bloke in Australia who's set up his own Twitter account to mimic mine and he copies the breakfasts.

I tweet about things that interest me and if I hear things that surprise me I'll throw it out into the Twittersphere to see what people think. Sometimes I'll be lying awake think-ing about something random, and I'll ask Twitter. The size of Cornettos, the price of Freddo Frogs, everything is game. I know you have to take everything you read on the internet with a pinch of salt, but it can be a useful way to find things out. I read a survey once that said almost 50 per cent of men from Germany sit down to have a piss. I was puzzled by this because I don't think I've ever had a sit-down wee, so I asked any German followers to confirm it. Judging by all the comments it was true, not just in Germany but also in the UK.

I get thousands of replies to my messages each day and it's impossible to go through them all individually, there just isn't enough time. One day I was in the van with Collins, and I'd posted something that went viral. The phone was buzzing so much with all the notifications it started to over-heat and I had to turn it off in case it set fire to the van. Mainly it's people saying, 'I needed that today, thank you, love your motivation' and sometimes it's people saying, 'Why the fuck are you eating that for breakfast?' The sunshine chicken curry with round chips always gets the biggest reaction, closely followed by spicy Korean noodles.

There is one comment that always sticks out in my mind and reminds me why I keep posting. A woman messaged me early one morning.

'Mr Skinner you have just saved my life,' she wrote. 'I was sitting there ready to kill myself. I have been working up to it for months and today was going to be the day. I'd written the letters for my family and I rang my best friend and told her what I was going to do. She told me that if I do one more thing I should look at your Instagram, so I spent two hours watching your videos. I'm still here. You've saved my life.'

That was a real lightbulb moment and made me realise that I have a responsibility to people because they do look forward to my posts. It's a duty and an honour. People are down, I try to pick them up. People need to be inspired, I'll try and inspire them. It's crazy, I motivate the nation one breakfast at a time.

If you ask me why I do it, I think it's down to who I am as a person and the way I am with my family and friends. I don't get down or stressed about things, and if there is ever a problem, I look for solutions, I'll always be positive. Because of that I'm generally the one my friends turn to for support and I'm always there for them and always happy to help. It is that attitude that filters through to the messages I send out on social media.

Although most of the interactions I have are positive, I still get trolls. Everyone does, it's part of life online. My advice to anyone who gets run down by keyboard warriors online is let 'em hate you then make them more jealous by being a success and doing things they could only ever dream of. They aren't worth your time or energy.

I won't lie, I like social media but it's not perfect. It can do a lot of good, but it can also be destructive, for example

I think it's killed the pub and nightclub trade because people used to go out and meet each other to have chats, now they just do it online, especially young people. The secret is not to take it too seriously. Get out of the house, meet real people, have a laugh. Want to be an influencer? Let's be honest, it's not really a proper job. Find something you love doing instead. That's why I still do the markets because I love it and I've done it all my life. I think if you lose touch with where you come from and who you are, you end up becoming a knob. Since being in this mad little industry I've met a lot of people who are famous for various reasons and a lot of celebrities. Most of them are really decent, but there are also quite a few who are absolute helmets and that's mad because they've got a persona when they're on telly but when the cameras stop, they turn into dicks. What's the matter with them?

Do I feel famous? I was always famous in Romford but I am the same person I've always been. Nothing's changed, except I've got a slightly nicer car and more than one suit now. I don't even know what I've done to get where I am. It just happened. People say I'm funny, but I don't try to be. I appeared in *8 Out of 10 Cats* with proper comedians and just talked normally. People laughed and clapped. I've done some big meetings with big brands and I just treat them like I'd treat a deal on a stall. 'Come on mate, I know you've got more money than that.' How am I the talent? I'm just a normal bloke.

# SKINNER'S SCRIPTURES

- Don't believe everything you see on TV.

- Don't believe everything you see on the internet.

- Stick up for injustice.

- Be fair with people.

## CHAPTER 10

# GIFT OF THE GAB

*'You can't be wrong
and strong.'*

LET ME TELL you a little story that I think you'll enjoy. It sums up the sort of situations I get myself into and most importantly, how I get myself out of them. The following is all true.

Years before I met my wife, when I was in my early twenties, I went on holiday to the Dominican Republic with a girlfriend I had at the time. I'd not done much long-haul flying, so it was a bit of an adventure. It was a spur of the moment booking. I'd had a couple of good weeks on the stall and banked a few quid which as usual was burning a hole in my pocket. It was January. Markets were slow and I fancied a bit of sunshine.

'We're going on holiday,' I announced.

'Where to?' she asked.

'Dunno, let's go see what deals are around.'

We looked online for winter sun breaks and most advertised the Canaries, which seemed a bit tame to me.

'Let's try the Caribbean,' I suggested.

Of all the destinations, the Dominican Republic looked suitable for our price range. I had no idea what it was like, but the photos of white sand and clear turquoise sea looked lovely.

'That's a bit of us,' I said. We started looking at hotel options. Most of them were all-inclusive, which suited me. I just fancied lazing around on the beach for a week, I wasn't arsed about taking in the local culture and going on excursions to museums or rum distilleries.

Most of the hotels were around £2,000, which was a bit over-budget, but one stood out as great value. It was only £700 and had several restaurants, two pools, its own private beach, a spa and fitness centre. I couldn't understand why it was so much cheaper than the others and glanced briefly over the reviews. Some said it was out of the way but that didn't matter to us as we were only there for a short while and unlikely to get bored, so we booked it and a week later found ourselves at the luggage carousel at the airport on the island picking up our bags and heading to the coach for the transfer. The air outside was so hot and humid it felt like being slapped in the face with a hot wet towel.

We found the bus that was taking us to the resort and got on it with the other people staying there. There was a man dressed in hotel uniform at the front of the bus but unlike other reps I'd seen on my holidays to the Canaries and Spain, he was carrying a rifle, which immediately made me suspicious. As the bus set off, the man with the gun started his welcome speech. It wasn't like other welcome speeches I'd heard.

'The hotel is stunning and has everything you will need,' he said. 'However, it is near the border with Haiti, which is dangerous. The hotel is perfectly safe and there is nothing to worry about, but outside the complex we cannot look after you so you should remain in the complex where you can enjoy everything we have to offer.'

At the time, Haiti was a lawless place. The country was very poor and corrupt. Kidnapping foreigners for ransom, particularly Americans, was a common problem and despite being in the Caribbean, it was not a tourist destination.

As the bus drove through the tall gates into the hotel complex, I could see guard huts on either side of the drive-way. The guards in them had machine guns. After we checked in and unpacked, we went for a stroll around the hotel complex. It was luxury and just like the photos showed. The armed guards dotted around the place and on the private beach seemed out of place in such an idyllic setting.

We relaxed into holiday mode and spent days on the beach and around the pool. Late one afternoon I fancied a massage, so I went to the spa in the hotel to see if they had any availability. It was around 5.30 p.m. and they apologised, told me they shut at six but explained that there was someone from the hotel in a hut on the beach who did massages until 7.30 p.m.

'If you go on the beach, turn left and walk right down to the end you'll find the massage hut,' I was told.

At about 6.30 p.m. we set off for a walk down the beach to find the hut. We went out, turned left and walked down the beach which was quiet by that point as the sun had started to set. There was no marker to signify the end of the hotel's beach, the sand stretched on for a couple of miles until the coast curved round so when it was busy, people just spread along the seafront and the guards patrolled the edges. We walked past one, a geezer with a gun on a chair, he didn't see us.

We carried on walking for about half a mile up the deserted beach.

My girlfriend got nervous.

'Are you sure we're going in the right direction?' she asked.

'This is where the lady in the spa told me to go. They've got to be down here somewhere,' I said.

We approached a line of large metal crosses jutting out the sand, like the type they use to stop tanks. There was barbed wire draped over them.

'We must be near the end of the hotel's part of the beach,' I said. 'It must be just around here somewhere.'

In hindsight, those barriers were probably the border between the Dominican Republic and Haiti. We carried on walking another few hundred yards until the sand turned to rocks. My girlfriend was imploring me to turn back but when it comes to directions I'm a typical bloke, I'd rather just keep going than admit I am lost or ask someone for help. We climbed over the rocks and onto a rough path that went into dense jungle.

'I think we've gone too far,' she said. 'Let's go back.'

It was dusk by now and I turned around and saw the lights of the hotel twinkling in the distance.

'We'll just have a look up this path and if it's not here we'll go back,' I said.

I hurried in front and a few yards ahead saw an opening with four scruffy shacks in it.

'They're here. I've found the massage huts,' I said and walked towards them.

We both emerged from the path into a compound littered with old bits of machinery and metal drums. In the middle on a chair sat a man with no legs. He was wearing a big gold necklace, had a whistle around his neck and was smoking a cigar. He didn't look like a masseuse.

'American?' he asked gruffly in an accent I couldn't place.

'No, London mate,' I answered.

'London?' he frowned.

'Yeah, London. England. You know. Queen. Buckingham Palace. West Ham? I'm looking for a massage.'

He looked really confused. Then he blew his whistle. Fuck knows why. All of a sudden other people came out of the huts. They looked at us menacingly.

My girlfriend started crying.

'What are you crying for? They're alright. They're locals, they love us,' I said to her. I turned to the men and explained, 'Listen guys, I'm after a massage. I've been walking for miles. The woman on reception told us to walk down here.'

One of the blokes nodded and beckoned for us to follow him. He led us into one of the shacks. It was dingy and sticky, there were flies buzzing around. It stunk of sweat and mould. There was an old, stained mattress on the floor and a door at the back leading into another sectioned off part of the structure. The door opened and a huge lady walked through it. She must have been 20 stone.

'Pay in dollars,' the geezer said, and walked out.

I realised that the woman was a prostitute, so did my girlfriend, who was next to me, still in tears.

'No! no!' I said. 'Listen love, no offence but I wanted a spa treatment, not a bunk up.' I reached into the bag slung across my chest and gave the woman $50, which would have been the equivalent of a couple of weeks' wages. Then I told her I was going. She held the money and said, 'I'll do everything for you.'

We made a quick exit. The geezer was waiting outside, he grabbed me and took me to another shack.

By this time, I admit I was getting nervous. I realised that we were in a dangerous situation and that these people could quite easily kidnap us or rob us, slit our throats and dump us in the jungle where we'd never be found. I needed to keep my cool and work a way out of the situation.

The man with no legs was inside the shack and we were both ushered in.

He was sitting at a table with a bottle of something pale on it and two dirty shot glasses.

'You drink with me,' he gestured. Then he poured out two glasses.

'This is mañana,' he said.

'What does mañana mean?' I asked.

'Tomorrow,' he said.

'Why, what's happening tomorrow?' I asked.

'You'll find out,' he replied and started laughing.

'Don't drink it. It might be poison,' my girlfriend said under her breath.

I looked at the bloke's gun, which was on his lap. I didn't really have a choice. I sniffed the drink and it smelt of rum, so I banged it back. It burnt the back of my throat but didn't taste of anything suspicious, just strong cheap liquor.

I put the glass on the table.

'Another,' I said loudly.

The bloke laughed and poured.

'This makes you strong like wood,' he said. I could tell he was starting to warm to me.

I downed another.

'We have something similar in England. It's called Aftershock,' I said. His face cracked into a smile of broken teeth, and he laughed. Then I started laughing. The other bloke in the room started laughing too. Even my girlfriend managed a smile. I could feel the atmosphere relax a notch.

Then the legless man stopped laughing and said, 'Now you give me your dollars.'

I had around $250 in my bag and this was the crux of it all. I was mad if I thought I could wander into the jungle compound of what looked like a band of pirates and walk out unscathed. They had guns, a 20-stone hooker and a mad leader with no legs and a whistle round his neck. These boys weren't messing around. We were being robbed and I knew that if I got away with losing just my money, I would be lucky. But some urge deep inside me refused to let me just stand there and get tucked up.

If he was going to take my money, which he obviously was because he and his mate had guns, I wanted something in return, just to make it seem a bit fairer.

'I can't give you that, I need more money for the rest of my holiday,' I said. Then I suggested, 'Why don't we have a trade instead?'

The leader thought about this for a minute, and I saw a look on his face that I'd seen a million times before. His eyes lit up at the thought of doing a deal. We might have been from different sides of the world and divided by different backgrounds and environments, but he recognised a fellow trader and there was a spark of connection. I'm not a big history buff but I do know that that's how civilisations expanded and developed throughout history. The first people to make connections were always the traders. A traveller from an unknown part of the world stumbles across a village somewhere and starts trading. Maybe he has some fur and the villagers are growing mangos and they both fancy doing a trade. That's how it all starts. It's like certain humans have an instinct to trade things. That's what happened in that shack in the jungle. That bloke saw a kindred spirit and the chance to have a deal. He would have robbed me, no doubt, but having a deal gave everyone honour.

'You like cigars, London?' he asked.

'I fucking love a la-di-da,' I said.

He gestured to his mate who went off somewhere and came back with a rusty old tin, that he handed to the legless bloke. He opened it dramatically in front of me. Inside were five fat cigars.

'Lovely,' I said. '$50?'

The bloke looked at me coldly.

'$250,' he demanded. I could tell the deal was non-negotiable.

I thought about it. '$250, but you throw in the mañana,' I said.

He stuck out his hand to shake. I noticed he was missing half his pinky finger. We shook, I counted out the money and picked up the cigars and the bottle, then said what a lovely time I'd had but that it was time for us to get back to the hotel and then we got the fuck out of there.

It was dark by then and we ran down onto the beach. My girlfriend was in tears again, probably in shock. We could see the lights of the hotel a mile away and ran towards them, not daring to look back. As we neared safety a hotel guard stepped out of the shadows and stopped us. We told him what had happened.

'Are you injured?' he asked. 'Did they torture you? Did they touch you?'

I told him we were okay and that we hadn't been assaulted.

'You need to talk to the authorities,' he said.

I told him that wasn't necessary.

'Anyway, I've got cigars,' I said, showing him the box. 'And a bottle of mañana.'

I don't think he could believe we'd escaped alive, and with souvenirs.

Why am I telling you this story? Well, apart from being one of the most unusual holiday stories you'll hear, it also illustrates a point I want to make, which is that having a laugh and a joke with people gets you a long way in life and can also get you out of all kinds of problems. There's a fine line of course. Don't take the piss out of people and don't make them the butt of your jokes, but if you can have a laugh with people, you can make them like you. And if they like you, you can do business with them.

This theory doesn't just work with amputee bandits in the jungle, it also works with gangster psychopaths. Let me explain.

Several years ago, a contact I totally trust rang me up and said he had a consignment of 2,000 bottles of this posh moisturising cream that sells for over £200 a pot. The labels on the pots had a tiny printing error on them, too small to be noticed by any normal consumer but it meant the manufacturer just wanted shot of them and my mate had bought the lot. They only sold this stuff in posh department stores.

'Do you know anyone who wants to buy it? It has to go as one package; it's a great price so I'm not dividing it up,' my mate said.

It was a high-cost parcel so I called my mate Gringo who had a network of contacts and asked if he could shift it. I rang round and tried to place it myself but the touch was too big, as they say, meaning it was too expensive for a lot of smaller traders I knew. Then one of Gringo's contacts made a call and reported back that he had a potential buyer, a bloke I'll call The Sergeant.

'Someone gave me his number and said speak to this geezer, he's fucking naughty, he runs it round here, he's the governor,' Gringo said. 'But for whatever reason he wants to buy the parcel.'

What Gringo was saying in our language was that The Sergeant was a proper big-time gangster. The type of man you wouldn't want to mess with or double cross. Normally he wasn't the type of person who would bother with ladies' cosmetics.

With this in mind, I got on the phone and prepared to do a fair and proper deal with the bloke. I didn't want any comebacks. We had a chat. To be fair, he seemed like a nice geezer. We agreed on a price. I called my mate, the seller, straight after and told him we'd have the parcel. It was one of those easy deals that doesn't happen too often. Gringo and me just acted as the middlemen. We bought the stuff from my mate, picked it up in the van, drove it to The Sergeant and sold it to him. For our troubles we earned several grand each.

The Sergeant was happy. He said he owned several beauty salons and he'd stock the gear in them, which explained why he was diversifying from his usual business, which I suspected involved extortion and felony crime. He shook our hands and said to call him if we came across anything similar.

We walked away laughing, with me thinking *fucking hell, that was easy.*

I did what I always tended to do after nicking a good few quid on an easy deal and spent it over the following weeks. So did Gringo.

Several weeks passed and I was in the pub, ironically with Gringo, when I got a call. I recognised The Sergeant's number. I thought maybe he'd sold all his stock and was looking for more.

'Alright mate,' I answered.

'I'm not your mate. I want a meeting with you and your boyfriend. I'm not happy,' he hissed.

I was confused.

'What do you mean?' I asked.

'I've got it on good information that the cream is fake,' he said.

Now I knew 100 per cent that the stuff was genuine. I had no doubt whatsoever.

'Well, it ain't. The bloke who got it is 100 per cent legit,' I explained.

'Don't argue with me c\*\*t. I know where you both live. I want all the money back tomorrow morning. If I don't get it back you are both getting ironed out,' The Sergeant breathed (ironed out meaning killed).

He was not the kind of person you want to hear those words from. He was not someone who made empty threats.

Gringo could tell by my face and what I was saying that there was a big problem.

'Speak to your mate, call me back and tell me where you're going to be tomorrow so I can get my money back,' he said, and then hung up.

I looked at Gringo and we both knew we were in trouble.

'Shit,' I said, 'What have you done with your money?'

'I spent it,' he said.

'So have I.'

I had a thought. 'This is what we do, we front it out and meet him somewhere where there are loads of people so he can't do anything. We'll talk to him and find out why he thinks it's fake, because I know that it's not.'

I knew a pub called The Shepherd and Dog in Romford which was always busy, and which had big windows at the front looking out onto the main road. It was a safe place to meet so I rang The Sergeant back and said we'd be there at 1 p.m. the following day, figuring it was always particularly busy at lunchtimes.

'Don't try anything silly, we're coming prepared,' he said threateningly.

The next day, after a sleepless night, I picked Gringo up and we went to the pub for our showdown.

Now normally the place was mobbed so we went an hour early to get the seats at the front in the window. Me and Gringo walked in and were the only two people there.

'This is fucking weird,' I said to him. 'I've never seen it as quiet as this.'

It was as if someone had told the pub to turn people away. We stood at the bar and there wasn't even anyone serving.

We went and sat in the window seats and waited for ages before an old man I didn't recognise came out from the back and took our orders. We ordered two burgers and two glasses of beer, meals for condemned men. I had a bad feeling about it and it's fair to say Gringo was bricking himself.

'This ain't good, we ain't got the money, we are fucked, they are going to iron us out, then they'll find our parents and iron them out too,' he said as he took a bite of his burger. His mouth was so dry he couldn't chew it properly and had to take a gulp of Stella to wash it down.

'Don't worry, I'll sort it,' I said.

Gringo shook his head. 'Tom, even you can't sort this one out.'

I reassured him that the goods were genuine and that I'd smooth things out.

We ate our food in silence and at 1 p.m. on the dot three black Range Rovers glided into the otherwise empty car park. They all had blacked out windows and identical number plates except for the last digit. It was like something out of a movie. At exactly the same time all four doors of each car opened and four geezers got out of each car. Every one of them was wearing a long black Mac.

'Fucking hell,' I breathed, 'Where's Guy Ritchie?'

'This ain't funny,' Gringo said.

The Sergeant was easy to spot. He was the oldest of them, in his fifties, and while all the others were big chunky goons with shaved heads he was thin, athletic, good-looking with slicked back hair and a big gold watch poking out from under his jacket, glittering in the sun.

He walked over to the pub with four other goons, while the rest stood around the cars and lit cigarettes.

The pub door opened, and The Sergeant strode in and walked straight over to us. Two of the goons stayed by the door, presumably to deter anyone from coming in and to stop us running out. The Sergeant sat down opposite me and next to Gringo. One geezer stood behind me, and the other behind Gringo.

The Sergeant tutted, shook his head, sighed dramatically and started talking.

'Don't flatter yourselves boys, these aren't for you, we've got a big meeting after this,' he said, gesturing to the muscle in the room. 'Long and short, I want the money back, I've had a think and I ain't a bully so I'm going to give you until the end of the week.'

I started to say something, but he cut me off.

'I don't want to hear that,' he shouted suddenly, which made me and Gringo jump.

I persisted.

'Mate, we've spent it,' I pushed.

The geezer behind me was glaring and twitching with his hand inside his jacket.

The Sergeant was getting angry. I raised my voice too.

'What's this geezer twitching for? Has he got a gun on him? Well fucking shoot me then.'

The Sergeant shouted louder.

'Shut your mouth Tommy and don't answer me back. I want the fucking money.'

We were having a proper row. It descended into shouting and Gringo sat there wide-eyed and shaking.

'The creams ain't snide. Who told you they were?' I demanded.

'That's none of your concern,' he said.

'Of course it is, they're lying, either that or they're a fucking idiot,' I said.

His face went red.

'Are you calling my old woman an idiot?' he spat.

Shit! I had to think quickly.

Every negotiation comes to a point where you have to put up or shut up. At that stage, having realised that it was his wife who was telling him the gear was snide, I could have defused the situation and rolled over, but I knew I was right and so I doubled down.

'She's wrong, 100 per cent,' I said. I had to stick by my guns, but this just made him angrier.

There we were in an empty Romford pub, me and Gringo, a psychotic gangster ready to erupt and two twitchy goons, probably with guns under their coats. *I've got to make this bloke laugh*, I thought to myself.

'Has anyone ever told you that you look like an older, better-looking Bradley Cooper?' I said.

Everyone stopped. The goons started sniggering and the bloke calmed down and cracked a tiny hint of a smile. It was like a little glint of sunshine in a pitch black room.

'You're a funny fucker Tommy,' he said.

I pushed the humour.

'But you do though, don't you?'

He was much calmer now.

'For fuck's sake Tommy, how big are your bollocks to be making jokes?'

'Fucking massive,' I said.

I don't think he could quite believe I was having a joke with him.

'You do know who I am don't you?' he asked. Which really means *you do know how dangerous I am, don't you?*

'Of course, I do, but we had a deal, and those creams were not snide. I have not sold you fake creams. Whoever told you they are is wrong, for whatever reason.'

'Okay,' he said, 'just suppose they are. How do we find that out?'

This was our chance to save our skins.

'Have you got any of the creams on you?' I asked. He did.

'Okay we'll take them to somewhere in town that stocks it and get them to verify it. I'll get in the car now. If the person in the shop says they're fake, I'll give you double the money back,' I offered.

Gringo looked at me like I was mad.

The Sergeant thought for a second and nodded.

'Sounds fair,' he said.

With that we got up and walked to the car park where I squeezed between two heavies in the back of the Range Rover The Sergeant was driving and Gringo got in the back of one of the other cars. We drove all the way to Central London and I tried to keep the banter going while thinking that at any point these guys were going to pull off down a lane and do me.

'Did you get a two-for-one discount on the coats?' I joked.

As we got further into town it got busier and I started to relax because there were less places to murder us without being spotted. Eventually the convoy pulled up outside a high-end department store. Me, The Sergeant and one of the heavies got out of the car. Gringo, who was white as a sheet, got out the car behind with another goon. We all walked into the store and into the cosmetics section where we found a counter which sold the cream. I asked The Sergeant for the pot and spoke to the lady behind the counter.

'Excuse me, I bought this from another store when I was on holiday and my wife reckons it's fake. You couldn't check and tell me if I've been stitched up could you?'

She was happy to oblige. She took the lid off. She looked at it carefully, sniffed it, dabbed a bit on her hand and rubbed it in.

'Of course it's genuine,' she said. Even though I knew it was, the relief was instant.

'Thanks love,' I said and took the pot back.

We walked outside in silence. I wasn't going to punch the air or anything.

I handed The Sergeant back his pot.

'I owe you a favour,' he said simply, then got in his car along with his muscle and drove off, leaving me and Gringo stranded in Central London but feeling like we'd just been given a reprieve from Death Row.

The whole event had been terrifying.

'I need a drink,' Gringo said.

We went to a bar and ordered champagne.

'Jesus Tom,' Gringo laughed. 'As soon as you started taking the piss and laughing with them they loved you.'

And that's the lesson. I fronted up to them and refused to back down because I knew I was right and I refused to be bullied. You can't be wrong and strong. But I also knew that the best way to get what you want is to make people laugh and make them like you. We could have carried on shouting at each other and eventually I would probably have been shot or beaten with a baseball bat. Chatting to them defused the situation and gave me a chance to talk my way out of it.

After the champagne, Gringo and I went to the Palm Beach Casino in Mayfair and started playing blackjack. Our lucky streak held, Gringo kept winning. We kept increasing our bets and ended up walking away with almost £50,000 between us. We cashed up the chips and went on a two-day bender in London. We did it all, champagne, steak, oysters. We booked rooms in a five-star hotel, I bought a Louis Vuitton bag, then lost it. We did the whole lot. Two days later we returned to Romford with nothing left but feeling like we'd been given a second chance.

My old man once said to me that if you can leave a room and people say 'he's a good man', you've done well in life. Don't worry about what people say about you, not everyone will love you, but find the ones who do like you and make them love you. I hope that at the end of our disagreement, The Sergeant felt a little bit of love for me.

# SKINNER'S SCRIPTURES

- Use humour to get yourself out of tricky situations, but don't take the piss.

- Make people laugh and they'll like you.

- If you know you are in the right, defend yourself.

- Stand up to bullies, but be careful if they have guns, whistles or goons.

- Check what time the spa shuts.

## CHAPTER 11

# AN ARMY MARCHES ON ITS STOMACH

*'Be the best version of yourself.*
*You do you.'*

'MIND, BODY AND spirit'. You've seen it written on a million fridge magnets. What does it mean? I'm not really the kind of bloke who goes on yoga retreats and I've never knowingly eaten a piece of tofu. Kombucha is not my thing, I'm more of a Lucozade Sport kind of guy – isotonic if you're asking. But I get the idea that it's no good having one without the other two. It's no good spending hours in the gym developing your body if you're unhappy with the rest of your life or if you are too anxious to talk to people. It's no good being super-healthy if you are not a nice person and no one likes you. It's no good being super-clever and being able to do the *Times* cryptic crossword if you're so fat you can't see your feet unless you look in a mirror.

So here I'm going to explain how I approach matters of mind, body and spirit and in doing so hopefully I can help you align your chakras and achieve a state of zen. Om!

# MIND: BOSH IS A STATE OF MIND

Bosh is more than just a word. It's a way of life. It's a proud announcement that something has been done well, it's a call to arms. I can't remember when I started saying bosh. Maybe it was one of my first words. 'Mamma', 'Dadda', 'Bosh!' It's just something that a lot of people in Essex say and it became like a catchphrase when I was on the markets. Sold something? Bosh! Done a deal? Bosh! Nicked a few quid? A-bosh! It's one of those words that means nothing and everything at the same time. I say it now without thinking. It makes people laugh and it describes my way of life. Hard work, mental toughness, having a laugh and standing on your own two feet. If you are struggling, there's only one thing to do and that's to be more bosh.

People look at me and the way I am, and they can be forgiven for thinking that I haven't faced any challenges because generally I'm happy all the time and I don't get stressed about things. But just because I'm a happy chappie doesn't mean I haven't had hardships. It's going through hard times and coming out the other end many times that have made me a tough, resilient person. In life you have to face challenges and you have to get through them in order to become strong. I have always been that person that everyone relies on. I have always been that rock that doesn't give up. In my circle of friends and family, if someone's having a bad day, they'll ring me to pick them up, help them or lend them money. I was like that as a kid. Even in the playground I was the one who stood up for everyone. I will always stick up for people. There's a scene in one of the *Only Fools And Horses* episodes where there's a riot. Del drives through the middle of it and everyone stops fighting to wave at him and say 'alright Del'. One of my mates says that's me. But really, it's the power of bosh. It has the power to unify everyone. It's like the East End version of the force in *Star Wars*. It is a wonderful thing to be in a position where you know you can cope with your own issues and help others with theirs. And you only get to that place by overcoming hard times.

One of the things I will say is that you don't have to have a plan. I never had a plan in my life, so I never worry about having to meet some target I've set myself, I never have to hurry to meet some self-imposed deadline. In fact, until I had my son I didn't really plan for the future. My philosophy was *live for the moment and if you lose it, go and get it again tomorrow*. I don't have loads of savings, not many people I know do. Money isn't something to be hoarded, it's something that's there to help me do what I need to do. Perhaps that's why I've always got to the brink of being a millionaire, but I've never got there. I've earned it but it's never hung around long enough to stick. And as for the flash stuff, of course I like it. Who doesn't like a flash car or a nice watch, but they are not priorities and to be honest, once you've had one flash car, all the others are the same.

I have faith in my ability to get by and I know that if times are hard, if I just push on, they'll get better one day. I guess you can call it self-reliance, rather than confidence. I'm not cocky. I know my limitations. I know I have faults just like we all do, but I accept them, I don't beat myself up about it and I make the best of every opportunity. Who knows how life will pan out? I don't, but I don't worry about it. I have a lovely family and great friends around me and that's the most important thing. The nice house and nice cars are a bonus but if they go, so be it. Family and friends are what matters because at the end of the day it's not all about money, it's about having love in your life, being loved and having experiences.

One of the surefire ways of being a success and of developing a bosh mindset is to surround yourself with decent people. Remember when you were young and your mum told you not to hang around Barry from down the road because Barry was no good, and you thought your mum was being a knob? Well, she knew what she was talking about. If you hang around with lazy people, or people who puff all day and don't work, or people who rob and have no manners, it all rubs off on you. When I think about my mates and all the people I've hung around with, they've all made something of themselves, even the ones who have been inside. You become who you hang around with. If I was to sit in the pub with the same old people talking the same old bollocks day in, day out, in ten years' time I'd still be in that same pub talking the same bollocks. But if I surround myself with people who go out and graft and do well, and there are loads around my manor, I'm like that sponge I talked about earlier. I'm picking up all their good habits. And I also want to keep up. If my mate is taking his missus to Smith's of Wapping for a long Saturday lunch and spending £300, I want to do that too and to do that I have to earn that money. Even if I'm lucky and the missus fancies a Nando's instead, I still have to earn enough in order to treat her to that wing roulette.

So, in a jumbled way, that's my mindset: the bosh way of life. And I know it's easy for me to say and that a lot of people have a really hard time with their mental health. I know it's a really big problem and if you are really struggling you need to talk to people and get help. There's no shame in asking for help, it shows you are strong.

Young people have a lot to contend with today and a lot of young people get anxious. I don't know why to be honest, I'm not a psychiatrist and I don't fully understand because it's not something I've ever had to deal with. The closest thing I've ever come to anxiety is a panic attack on a plane and that was just a temporary thing. I understand why it happens, but I still can't help myself because I have a fear of flying.

The worst incident happened when I was coming back from Dubai once with Sinéad. I'm a terrible flyer anyway, I literally scream when we take off or go through turbulence. I must be the worst person in the world to travel with. On this particular flight Sinéad was watching a movie and relaxing and I was sitting in the seat sweating as usual, grabbing the armrest and sinking my nails into it with every jolt of the plane. I looked over towards the toilets and galley where the emergency doors were and I saw two men standing there, talking loudly to each other. They were having an argument. It's not what you want to see on a plane. You want everyone to be calm. I continued staring at them and one of them glanced over at me, then carried on arguing. The longer I looked at them, the more convinced I got that they were up to something. Sweat started pouring off me. My heart started racing. I started breathing hard as adrenaline flooded through me.

My mind was racing. *I've got to do something, they're going to kill us all, these slags are going to open the door.* By then I was totally paranoid, and I got up and walked over to them.

'Sit down, I know what you're doing, sit the fuck down!' I shouted at them.

They looked at me like I was mad, which I was.

Sinéad saw what was happening and came over to try and calm me down.

'Come on Thomas, you know how you get on planes. Come and sit down.'

But that was it. It's hard to explain but it felt like I was possessed. I wasn't capable of rational thought. I was absolutely convinced they were going to take the plane down.

I got more agitated.

'We have to land the plane!' I shouted.

Sinéad managed to calm me down and coaxed me back to the seat. There was a nurse sitting behind me and she said, 'Sir, I think you're having an anxiety attack.'

'No I'm not, there's something wrong with the plane!' I screamed. I couldn't understand why no one was taking me seriously.

'Those geezers have got a bomb. I'm going to fly the plane.' I was delirious.

It all went a bit blurry after that because my body was flooded with adrenaline, and I started to hyperventilate, but at some point an Air Marshall showed up and took me out of my seat and to the back of the plane where I was strapped into a seat with a belt that had no buckles on it so I couldn't undo it. A doctor arrived and gave me gas and air and then I was conked out with Valium for the rest of the flight. When we landed, they checked I was okay and let me go. They were very understanding. I hadn't been drinking, it was genuinely a panic attack. Sinéad came and got me. Luckily she knows what I'm like and is very laid back so she was able to tell the crew that I had a history of fear of flying.

But my anxiety over flying is nothing compared to people who suffer real anxiety all the time over normal things like going out and socialising. People do suffer and we all go through hard times. Sometimes in life you've just got to push yourself to get through things, you've got to get above and beyond it. As hard as it may seem and as dark as it may seem, hard times won't last, and you can crawl your way out of it. The only way you can do that is to surround yourself with good people.

When you are young, take the knocks. People worry about what they look like, what they have, how many likes they've got. Who gives a fuck? When I go to work, I don't care what I look like but it's horses for courses, if you are going to a wedding you can't turn up in a pair of tracksuit bottoms. Make sure you have a bath or shower but otherwise don't get caught up comparing yourself to people you see on TV or on Instagram. Concentrate on building core values of politeness, manners, loyalty and hard work. Be genuine. Be trusting but don't be a mug because some people will have an agenda; when you find them out, shut them out. Find something you love. Enjoy life, have a healthy balance. There's not much more to it than that.

# BODY: A BACON ROLL AIN'T GONNA CUT IT

As the proud proprietor of Bosh Gyms, I can say hand-on-heart that exercise helps keep you sane. Health is important because you can have all the money in the world but if you can't walk up the stairs, or you can't kick a ball around with your kids, what good is any of it? Health and happiness. That combination is the key to life.

You don't have to smash the gym every day or run 10k each morning but make sure you take some form of exercise several times a week, even if it's just a walk or bike ride.

Modern life is all set up to make you fat. That's a fact. Everything at eye level in the shops, everything by the tills, all the stuff in the petrol garage, it's all designed to kill you slowly. I know I sound like a conspiracy theory nutcase but in the case of food, it's true. Your body is designed to crave high-calorie, high-fat, high-sugar foods and the big food companies know this so they place those items where you will see them and sell them to you when you are most susceptible. Trying to live a constant healthy lifestyle is so hard because all the cards are stacked against you. I know because it's a struggle I have every day. I love my food, I love all the things that are bad for me – chocolate, beer, McFlurries – and I haven't got the willpower to resist most of the time. But what I can do is exercise to at least alleviate some of the effects.

Now I know what you're saying. *Mate, we've seen what you eat for breakfast. You're in no position to tell us to cut our calories.* And you'd be right, but let me defend myself for a moment. I have a monster breakfast because I start grafting at 5 a.m. going to the yard, loading the van, setting up the stalls. In the winter, it's freezing cold. A bacon sandwich just ain't gonna cut it. To fuel that kind of activity until lunch (which is generally a sarnie) you need to get to Dino's and get yourself a slab of lasagne for breakfast or the spicy Korean noodles with chicken and two poached eggs, or the sunshine chicken curry with the round chips, or even the steak and kidney pie with steamed veg and mashed potato. And remember, don't look when you pour the gravy.

These are the meals that set you up for the day. Anyone who gets up early and grafts recognises this. Bricklayers, delivery drivers, scaffolders; what do you reckon they'd say if you offered them a bowl of overnight oats and some fruit? Exactly.

So yes, I do eat mental breakfasts, but for a reason. Normally I eat three meals a day but if I'm really busy and running all over the place and have had a training session with Hughie in the morning in the gym, I might have a cheeky McDonald's in the afternoon. I do try to cut back sometimes, especially when the old double-chin starts to show up. I've tried fasting, I've dieted, and Sinéad is brilliant because she'll cook me healthy stuff and then I've got to eat it. But the problems come at night after a beer. That's when I started on the Cornettos and the Cadbury's Picnics.

If you ask me what my death row final meal would be, that's an easy one. A nice steak, medium rare, dauphinoise potatoes and peas, and for dessert it's got to be sticky toffee pudding, custard and a little side of ice cream. Vanilla or pistachio, I'm not fussy.

My love of grub ended up getting me on *MasterChef*. They rang me up and invited me to be a contestant. Although I could cook, I'd never done any of that fancy stuff before so one of my dad's mates who has a restaurant in Leigh-on-Sea offered to show me the ropes. For a few evenings one week before I started on the show, I went to his place and worked in the kitchen. It was a fine-dining establishment, and I prepared dishes like scallops with oyster mushroom sauce and sauteed potatoes. I learned how to fillet a fish and slice and batter it. I learned to slice and dice vegetables properly. By the time I started on the show, I knew what I was doing and I got into the semi-final. The whole thing was filmed over a few weeks, and I enjoyed doing it. I learned a lot too.

It was a proper competition and although I'm quite competitive, as I didn't know so much about cooking, I listened to the advice and treated it as a learning experience. My signature dish was battered fish and chips. I made my own tartare sauce and made an apple tart with caramel sauce. It was during that show the famous 'I don't get nervous' meme was created.

In one task we were cooking food for a function for the charity Guide Dogs for the Blind. John Torode decided he was going to wind me up to make things a bit interesting for the cameras and he kept coming up to my station and digging me out for no reason.

'Thomas, you need to cook it for a bit longer.'

'Thomas, the oven's on.'

He was winding me up and I had a mic on which I forgot. When he walked away under my breath I muttered something like, *say that one more time I'll put your head in the oven*. All the crew heard it and pissed themselves laughing.

## SPIRIT: TRUST YOUR GUT

I'm going to throw in a bit in the end about spirit not because I'm massively religious or spiritual – I'm not into crystals and dreamcatchers and Himalayan salt lamps – but because I do believe that we have a sixth sense that we can feel things through. Call it premonition, psychic ability, I don't know, but what I do know is that I get premonitions and feelings about things that are about to happen, and they usually turn out to be true.

My whole life I've been able to predict outcomes of things before they happen. It is weird. I can sit in a pub, and I'll turn to Sinéad and say, 'We need to leave here, it's going to kick off in a minute.' All of a sudden, there'll be a fight.

I can sense energy. I know when it's going to be a good or bad day on the market. There have been mornings when it's pissing down with rain and Collins or Big Lanks will say, 'Come on, let's sack this off, we're wasting our time.' And I'll say, 'We've got to stay. It will be a good day.' And then the sun comes out, loads of punters turn up and we smash it. Basically, I think I might be a fortune teller, I've unlocked my third eye.

I can read people. I can tell if someone is trying to have one over on me. I've warned mates about people and six months down the line they've been stitched up by them. I sensed one mate's girlfriend was a wrong 'un and told him from day one, *I don't know what it is, but I know she ain't good for you.* We ended up falling out. He married her. I didn't go the wedding and a few years later he apologised because it turned out she was having an affair behind his back for four years and robbed all his money.

You might not believe it, and sometimes I don't either because I'm very sceptical about things, but I think we all have an ability to read the energy around us, like when you walk into a room and you just get a bad feeling. Some people are more sensitive to it than others.

For example, I just knew Sinéad was having twins when she got pregnant the second time. We were sitting on the sofa one evening and she said to me she wasn't showing like she did with our first, Henry. Without thinking about it I said, 'It's because you're having twins.' I just knew it.

She didn't believe me.

'It's impossible,' she said. 'There are no twins in either of our families.'

'I'm telling you now, we are having twins,' I said.

It was left at that until we went for the first scan a few weeks later. The woman rubbed the jelly on her belly and I looked at the big plasma screen TV and I could see clear as day two babies on the screen and I thought, *I fucking knew it*. How do you explain that?

I'll finish this bit with the only religious story I can think of. It won't be particularly enlightening to be honest, and it doesn't tell you anything about the meaning of life, but it's funny, and that's what counts.

I have a mate, Big Dean. He's a body builder. He is one of life's lovely people and I've known him for years. We'd often meet up for a beer and sometimes we trained together in the gym, which is where we were one afternoon a few years ago when we decided that we'd finish up and go for a pint.

When Dean trains, he trains hard, which means he sweats. I, on the other hand, lift the odd dumbbell, wipe my forehead and talk to people.

So, we're in the gym and Dean is giving it large with the free weights. When he finished he was dripping so we decided to pop back to his place in Gidea Park where he could have a shower and change. I didn't need to because I am a lightweight.

'We'll go back to mine, I'll have a shower, leave your car there and we'll have a few pigs ears,' he said.

As we pulled up at his house, Dean explained to me that his auntie was calling round.

'If she knocks while I'm in the shower, can you let her in?' he asked.

'Of course,' I said.

I made myself at home in the kitchen and put the kettle on to make a cup of tea and before it boiled there was a knock on the door.

*That must be Dean's auntie*, I thought to myself and went to open it.

On the doorstep stood two well-dressed ladies. One was older, one was younger. Both of them were holding packs of pamphlets.

'Come in,' I said, opening the door for them and stepping aside. 'Dean's in the shower.'

They glanced at other quickly and then walked inside.

'I'm Dean's mate, Tom,' I offered. 'I've just put the kettle on, do you want a cup of tea?'

They followed me back into the kitchen and said yes, tea would be nice.

While I was making us all a drink, I started making idle conversation.

'We've just been to the gym, you know what Dean's like with his big guns. He got sweaty so he's had a shower, I didn't need one.'

The women both looked at me nodding their heads. They weren't saying much.

'How's your day been?' I asked.

The older one spoke.

'Quite good actually, how's yours?' she said.

'Can't complain,' I said. 'I'm looking forward to a couple of beers.'

The older one frowned.

'Do you drink?' she asked.

'Course I do love,' I laughed.

Then from out of nowhere she asked me what I thought about God.

*That's a strange thing to ask*, I thought, but I wasn't going to be rude because she was Dean's aunt.

'Er, you know, whatever makes you happy,' I managed.

Then she whacked out a questionnaire and started asking about my faith. Did I pray? Did I go to church? Did I believe there was something bigger out there? Did I ever question my existence? It was getting a bit weird but you have to respect people's values so I went along with it and answered her as best as I could.

Even weirder, the younger girl never said a word, just looked at me.

I was quite relieved when I heard Dean's footsteps coming down the stairs. He walked into the kitchen and did a double take. He looked at the two women, looked at me and frowned. They looked at him and smiled politely.

'Tom,' he said, 'who the fuck are these people?'

'Your aunt and your niece?' I asked.

'No,' he said.

I turned to the women.

'Who are you?' I asked.

The older one answered for them.

'We're Jehovah's Witnesses,' she said. 'We have an important message we would like to share with you.'

Dean started laughing.

'I'm really sorry,' I said. 'I thought you were his auntie.'

'That's okay, but while we're here why don't you let us tell you our good news message?' she replied.

I glanced at Dean. This was eating into drinking time. I felt bad so I carried on talking to them for another awkward ten minutes while they told us the end of the world was coming but the good news was that true believers will be okay.

'I hope it doesn't happen before last orders,' I joked.

Eventually we politely decline their offer of conversion and asked them to go because we had an appointment with the Lord of lager. They left us some pamphlets in case we changed our minds.

# SKINNER'S SCRIPTURES

- Be more bosh.

- Surround yourself with people you admire and want to be like.

- Be thankful for what you've got.

- Focus on health and happiness.

- Trust your intuition.

- Beware of strangers bearing pamphlets.

## CHAPTER 12

# FAMILY FORTUNES

*'Fortune favours the brave.'*

WHEN I SEE an opportunity, I go for it. You have to because the rewards can be massive. The best opportunity I ever took wasn't on a deal, it was on my wife, Sinéad. I saw her at a bar late one afternoon and I thought, *she's a bit of me.* The story of how we met is a typical example of why you should always take a risk and have a go, because if you don't try, you'll never know.

Let me set the scene for you. As I've said before, my life has been full of ups and downs, booms and busts. I was in one of my bust phases. I'd been running an investment firm raising money for stocks and shares and I wasn't very good at it. I was living back with my mum temporarily and was in the City of London having a meeting with my bank manager in order to try and persuade him to extend me a line of credit which I needed to keep the business afloat.

I was wearing a shirt, tie and waistcoat in the hope that appearing business-like might trick the bank manager into looking past my balance sheet.

'Have you bought your business plan, Mr Skinner?' the geezer asked.

'It's in my head,' I explained.

It was quite obvious I was trying my luck. The bank manager levelled with me.

'You don't have any paperwork and no business plan. You have £1,050 left in your account and we are thinking about shutting it,' he said. 'You've obviously tried your best but sometimes things don't work out no matter how hard you try. We can't really carry this on.'

I had to agree.

'Okay,' I nodded. 'Give me the £1,050 and close the account.'

He went to the cashier's desk, counted out the cash and handed it to me in a white envelope which I folded and tucked into my pocket, where it immediately started burning a hole.

Now some people would have walked out of that situation with their head hung low feeling like a failure. The business had gone down the pan after all. But not me. I walked out with a skip in my step. It was a busted flush. I needed to lance the boil and get on with something else. An end is a beginning of something else, after all. And to add to the excitement, I had just over a grand in my pocket and nothing to do for the rest of the day. It was late afternoon and I decided to head to a bar to celebrate.

I was near St Paul's and headed to a place called Happenstance, which ironically is on the same square as the restaurant where they filmed the Channel 4 series *First Dates*. Thanks to its location and the fact it was Thursday night, which is the busiest night in the City, the Happenstance was full of city brokers, and quite a few were loud, rude and arrogant. I know there are plenty of nice ones but it is one of those professions where you find helmets. Nonetheless I strolled up to the bar, pushed through a gaggle of braying city boys and ordered a beer.

I took a long mouthful of lager, looked around and then stopped. At the other end of the bar, I spotted a beautiful girl who was chatting with her mate. She was smartly dressed and fit with soft features and long brunette hair. I walked over and introduced myself.

'Full of knobheads in here, ain't it? Can I buy you a drink?'

I bought them a drink and we started chatting and having a laugh, taking the piss out of the city boys. I found out her name was Sinéad and that she worked as a secretary at an environmental firm nearby that checked soil for contamination in building sites. She lived in North London with her parents. I told her I was a business owner from Essex and was in London for a meeting with my bank manager. I didn't tell her the business had folded and the money in my pocket was everything I had. I didn't care about that because I knew I'd be out at the weekend back on the markets earning more.

After a few drinks, her mate was getting ready to leave so I said, 'They're all mugs in here, do you want to come out with me tonight?'

Sinéad wasn't sure because she had to be in work the next morning.

'Come on, live a little,' I urged.

She looked at me and thought about it.

'You're not a murderer, are you?'

'Not yet,' I laughed.

She pointed out that it was totally out of character for her to go off with someone she'd just met, but I assured her we'd just have a few drinks and that would be it.

'Okay, just a couple of drinks,' she said.

'I promise, I'll look after you,' I said.

We got a black cab, and I asked the driver to take us to a place called Sushi Samba which is a bar and restaurant high up in Heron Tower, one of London's skyscrapers. It has the highest outside terrace in Europe, and you get to it via a glass elevator on the outside of the building. The cab fare was only £5 and we could have walked but I wanted to impress this girl.

I didn't let on when we stepped in the lift that I'm scared of heights and hugged the side as we glided up into the city skyline. At the top we got out and walked into the restaurant where the maître d' knew me and got us seats at the busy terrace bar.

Sinéad was explaining about her job and to be honest I didn't have a clue what she was talking about. I told her about myself and that I ducked and dived for a living. She thought I was mad. I made out I had a few more quid than I did.

The hours flew by. We finished off a bottle of wine and by then we were pissed and I was flirting. She was laughing and I thought I was in.

Neither of us had eaten and it was getting on a bit. I didn't want the night to end so I asked if she wanted to go and get a bite to eat.

'It's good in here but let me take you somewhere a bit special,' I said.

By that point in the evening the wine and my banter had persuaded her I wasn't a murderer and she agreed, so we ended up in another cab heading to Little Italy in Soho where I know the owners very well as I'd been going there since I was 15.

The place was heaving. There are two of the biggest, ugliest bouncers on the door who both knew me, shook my hand and ushered me in. They could see I had a girl with me and put on a bit of a performance.

'Tommy! Lovely to see you. How are you? Please come in.'

Once inside the owner came over and played along.

'Tommy, great to see you. As you can see we are full, but we can sort you out a table.'

He asked two waiters to bring a table from out the back which they did. They got the chairs and a tablecloth and set a table especially for us. I ordered a bottle of Laurent Perrier Rosé.

The restaurant puts on entertainment and there's a magician who wanders between tables doing tricks. He came over and started doing his magic. I was having the time of my life, throwing fifties around, giving it large.

'I'm gonna take you all over the world, darling,' I said to Sinéad. 'Me and you are going to have amazing times.'

I didn't tell her I was living with my mum.

Still, we had the best night and we shared a little snog.

By that point all intentions of an early night had long since vanished. I asked her if she fancied a dance and she did, so off we went to the club at 100 Wardour Street. By that stage my tie was off, my shirt-tails were hanging out my trousers, I had her make-up smeared on my cheek, wine all over me and chocolate on my shirt, but I also had my dancing shoes on and we hit the dancefloor, smooching and moving, not caring what else was happening around us or what people thought.

All too soon it was 2 a.m. and time to leave. In my drunken optimism I thought I'd be heading back to Sinéad's place. We left the club and the air hit me.

'Right, let's get a cab back. Finsbury Park, right?' I remembered that was where she lived.

I put my hand in my pocket and pulled out one £20 note.

That was all I had left from my £1,050. I knew the fare to her home would be around £15 so I hailed a cab and she gave the driver her address. I assumed I'd be staying with her so the score would just about see me right.

We pulled up outside and she went to get out of the cab. I followed. She turned to me, gave me a kiss and said, 'Thank you Thomas, I've had a lovely night.' And then she walked away, leaving me standing there, the cab behind me with the engine running and the driver in the front waiting for his money.

*Shit*, I thought, *that didn't go to plan.*

I turned to the driver and he raised an eyebrow. He'd seen it a million times.

'Thought you were going in, did you mate?' he said.

'Yeah,' I said. 'Now, the problem is I've only got £20 on me and I need to get back to Romford.

'That's about £50 from here,' he said.

I told him the truth. I confessed that I'd given it Larry Large and done a grand trying to impress the girl and now had less than a tenner left. I promised that if he ran me back to Romford and gave me his details I'd pay him back the next day.

He laughed.

'Mate, you're in luck. I was clocking off anyway and live in Ilford, I'll take you home,' he offered.

He was a saint and all the way back I bored him, telling him that Sinéad was the one.

'The amount of people who say that in the back of my cab,' he laughed. On the way Sinéad texted me to say thanks again and I told her I'd love to take her out again.

I got back to my mum's place where I was sleeping on the sofa, went to sleep, woke the next day and texted Sinéad to see if she wanted to go out that night. *Sure*, she messaged back, *where do you want to go?*

*Cinema?* I suggested.

That day I had to go out grafting in the van to earn a few quid and I picked her up straight from work wearing a tracksuit and driving a 15-year-old rusty van with holes in the seats and a piece of string to pull the windscreen wipers with, because the motors on them didn't work.

'Where's your Ferrari?' Sinéad asked.

'In the garage,' I joked.

We went to Nando's, Hollywood Bowl and then the cinema where I nicked the pick and mix because I hardly had any cash.

In two nights, Sinéad got to see the different sides of my life, the boom and bust, and she stuck by me. She's very grounded and laid back and doesn't care whether we go to the best restaurants or a £10.99 all you can eat Chinese buffet. She's the perfect one for me.

We started courting and on another of our early dates, after I'd had a good week trading, we ended up having a drink and a party with a group of mates back in Little Italy.

It was another one of those mad nights. I bought a massive bottle of vodka that you couldn't lift so you couldn't pour it and we got a table in the upstairs club where we were laughing and dancing. For some reason a circle of blokes on another table took a dislike to our party and one of them, a big bloke with a shaved head, came over to my mate Warren and ordered him to 'stop dancing around like you run the gaff'.

'Carry on like that and we'll fill you in,' he threatened.

Granted, Warren isn't the best dancer in the world but there was no need for that.

I hadn't seen this happening because I was talking to Sinéad and Warren came over to me and said that we'd better calm down.

'That lot over there are getting tasty,' he said, pointing to the table of geezers, who I have to admit, did look like proper gangsters.

I went to smooth things over.

'No aggro mate, we're just having a drink and a laugh,' I said.

One of them stood up and faced me.

'Your mate is a flash fucker. If you carry on messing around, see my pal over there,' he gestured to the biggest bloke in the group, a round hulk of a man with no neck and a head like a huge thumb, 'he's going to come over there and break your fucking nose.'

They were all looking agitated and jumpy, with wide eyes, and I realised they must have been bingeing on cocaine.

I went back to our group and thought *fuck it, I'm not going to be pushed around by these muppets.* We carried on laughing and joking and out of the corner of my eye I saw the big bloke striding across the floor heading for Warren, fists clenched. I knew what he intended to do so before he could get to Warren, I stepped in front of him and hooked him as hard as I could on the side of the jaw. He went five feet sideways headfirst into a table where two people were having dinner. Soup and spag bol went everywhere and people started screaming.

I turned to the fat geezer who started it all and said, 'Do you want one as well?'

By the look on his face he didn't.

Within seconds three doormen came running up the stairs, grabbed me and started hauling me out.

Sinéad, who had taken all of this madness in her stride, then said the immortal line.

'Don't throw him out, I really like it here, the music's great.'

And that's why I love her.

As it happened, I didn't get thrown out, but we did have to leave sharpish because the doormen told us they were indeed 'known' people and we should make ourselves scarce. Besides, they had to call an ambulance for the bloke I knocked out, who was also missing several teeth that were later found by a cleaner under a radiator.

Sinéad soon got the measure of me. If I'd had a good

week, it was Mayfair and the West End; if I had a bad week, it was the cinema and Nando's. After about two months of courting, I nicked myself ten grand out of a deal so I took her for three nights to a swanky London hotel. By the third night I'd done all my money and Sinéad had to pay. We moved in together about a year after that.

When we were together, I went out and bought a Tempur pillow because I was having trouble sleeping. It was £90 which I thought was steep at the time but honestly, it was the best pillow I ever had, and I wouldn't shut up about it with my mates and with Sinéad.

'Tom, it's just a pillow,' everyone would say. But I was obsessed, and I did what I'd done with the mattresses and found a manufacturer who had a look at it and told me it would cost £8 or £9 to make.

Everyone needs a pillow, I thought, this is a no-brainer. But I needed money to start the business so I went to my mate, Big Mark, who always helped me out and asked if he'd like to invest ten grand in my new pillow business.

'Tom,' he said, 'you're about as reliable with money as a sieve. You ain't having ten grand of mine, but I'll come in as a partner with you.'

So Big Mark, a lovely man who is tragically no longer with us, helped me buy my first lot of pillows and they sold well. It became The Fluffy Pillow Company, the reason Sinéad eventually applied to *The Apprentice* for me.

So, me walking into that bar and spotting her all those years ago led directly to where I am now. They say that behind every good man is an even better woman and they are right. We got married on 21 May 2022 and I couldn't have been prouder to say I do.

I became a father to my son Henry in October 2020. When Sinéad let me know she was pregnant I thought it was a wind up. Not because I didn't want to be a dad, I was over the moon, it was the way she did it, which was actually very lovely.

Sinéad was at work when she did the pregnancy test and had a do to go to that evening. When the test was positive, she wanted to get home and tell me so made an excuse and told her colleagues I'd lost my keys and she needed to get home to let me in.

Before she left, she wrote a note: 'To Daddy, I can't wait to meet you, love from Baby Skinner.' She put it in an envelope with the positive pregnancy test.

She got home before me and when I got in, she handed over the envelope which was addressed to me and said someone had put it through the letterbox earlier. I opened it and read it. I stood there for a minute trying to work it out. My first thought was *what the fuck is this*? It took me a minute to work it out but when the penny dropped, I was ecstatic. I'd always wanted to be a dad and have a family of my own and there we were, starting out on that adventure.

Knowing I was going to be a father was a wake-up call. I knew I needed to be more responsible and more sensible with money because I had people who depended on me. The pregnancy coincided with the pandemic and during lockdown I grafted hard while Sinéad grew our baby. We came out of lockdown and the world started to adjust to living with Covid. There were so many rules and restrictions, and I wasn't allowed into some of the appointments because hospitals were stopping partners attending.

Sinéad's due date in October came and went and when she was 12 days late the hospital called her in to induce her. It happened just at the time the Government announced there was going to be a second lockdown at the start of November.

The rule at the hospital was that dads were only allowed in once 'active labour' had started. I had to drop Sinéad off at the hospital entrance and go off and wait for the call. It was horrible not being able to be there with her, but she's a strong girl and I knew she'd be okay and was in safe hands.

A few hours later I got the call no dad-to-be wants to hear. Sinéad was in tears on the other end of the line.

'It's not good news, the baby is upside down and its heartbeat has dropped.'

For the first time I heard a real panic in Sinéad's voice, and I felt completely helpless. It was horrific, I just wanted to be there with her.

'I'm coming there, hang on babe.'

'You're not supposed to come in,' she sobbed.

'I need to be there with you,' I said.

And that was it. I went straight to the hospital because I couldn't see what the difference was between being there when the labour started and being there now, when her and the baby were in trouble. If they had to do an emergency caesarean I wanted to be there and frankly, no one was going to stop me.

I got to one of the entrances of the hospital and there was a security guard on the door.

'You can't come in,' he said.

I was in no mood to mess around.

I said, 'Mate, I'm going to drop £50 on the floor when you walk over there,' basically telling him to turn his back. He understood.

'I might lose my job?' he protested.

'Do you want £50 or not?' I said.

Evidently, he did, because he walked away. I dropped the money and I walked straight in. There was no one inside. As I walked through, I saw an apron hanging on the back of a door and I grabbed it and a surgical mask that was hanging with it, put them on and walked all the way through to maternity. No one stopped me. I found Sinéad on the ward. She looked white as a sheet. I gave her a hug.

'How did you get in here?' she asked.

'You know me,' I shrugged.

I sat with her for a while and she explained that they were monitoring the baby's position and heartbeat and were worried that the cord might be wrapped around its neck.

A nurse came into the room and looked at me.

'You are not meant to be here,' she said.

'Well, I'm here now,' I said.

She started laughing. I think she understood that there was no point trying to turf me out again.

I started having a laugh with the other nurses and they let me stay. Soon after that Sinéad started having contractions anyway, so I was officially allowed to be there.

I noticed a girl sitting opposite and she looked in a bad way. She had no possessions, no one was with her, and I could see the signs that suggested she was probably an addict.

Having established that I was allowed to be there, and that Sinéad was okay and the baby was stable, I took the opportunity to pop out to a shop and stock up on goodies for everyone. I bought back bags of Percy Pigs and cakes.

The labour continued and Sinéad was closely monitored. I was allowed to stay overnight and the next morning I popped out again to get everyone anything they needed. I also got nappies and wipes and other baby stuff for the woman opposite who looked like she needed it.

The contractions continued and we were moved to the delivery suite. And that's when things went south rapidly. Sinéad was struggling and the midwives and doctors were constantly monitoring her. I could see they were worried about something. At one stage one of them pushed an emergency button to call the specialist who came, checked everything and then pulled me out of the room and took me to one side.

'There's a complication,' she said. 'The cord is around the baby's neck, he's being strangled. It's 50/50 because he's upside down as well. We need to get him out now or he will die.'

I listened, trying to stay cool, automatically shovelling Percy Pigs into my mouth from the bag I'd been carrying around with me. Sinéad didn't know any of this.

'Do you want to tell Sinéad?' the doctor asked. I thought it would be best if she didn't know the full extent of the danger the baby was in.

'Don't worry Mr Skinner, I'm going to get this baby out,' the doctor said with a determined look on her face.

She controlled the situation like a god. I was in awe. She directed everyone to do what they needed to do in order to deliver the baby and orchestrated the birth like a conductor in a classical concert.

Sinéad was in awful pain and by the time they called for an epidural it was too late to administer it, so she had to go through the whole thing with just gas and air.

They used forceps and the doctor managed to manoeuvre Henry around, so he came out without being strangled.

I was there eating Percy Pigs as he was pulled out.

The first time I saw him he was purple and his head was the wrong shape. My heart sank, he was motionless and floppy. *He's dead*, I thought. Then the doctor smacked his back and suddenly he let out a snuffling sound and then started to cry. It was the sweetest sound I've ever heard.

Once he'd been cleaned up, given a quick check over and handed to Sinéad I hugged the doctor. I was overcome.

'That was close,' she said.

Sinéad and Henry were monitored for the next few hours to make sure they were okay. Because of Covid the hospital wanted to get people out as soon as they could, so we were allowed to go back home that afternoon. I carefully put Henry in his carrier and clipped him into the car for the first time and drove my new family back to the house. I don't think I've ever driven so slow or so carefully.

Sinéad was exhausted and needed to sleep so I told her to get her head down. I'd take care of the baby. She was out in seconds.

I took Henry into the lounge and laid him down on his mat. I took a long look at him and was hit by a wave of emotion. I started crying because I didn't know what to do, but I knew I had to look after him.

When I pulled myself together, I picked him up and we had a chat.

'I'm going to look after you son,' I said. 'You be a good boy and we'll have lots of adventures together.'

The first few weeks of parenthood were madness. No one tells you what it's like and even if they do you can't really appreciate it until you've done it. You can get all the advice in the world and read all the books to prepare, but you learn on the job. Half the time you don't really know what's happening, you just get through it.

I didn't have the luxury of being in a job where I get paternity leave and holiday pay so I had to go back to work quickly to get the money in, but I loved coming home to my family every night.

We are just a normal family. We like cooking a bit of dinner together and you've probably seen the videos. Sinéad is behind the camera filming me. She's a great cook and tells me what to do. I usually start the meal and she usually finishes it off.

I'm quite spontaneous so we tend not to make plans. If I get home early, we'll go out for lunch, which is one of the advantages of having a job that isn't 9 to 5. Our favourite things to do are chilling out indoors and having friends round.

When I started writing this Sinéad was eight weeks pregnant with our twin daughters. Things were busy. I was doing more TV and radio work while still grafting. Loads of opportunities were coming my way. One of them was the biggest of my life.

# SKINNER'S SCRIPTURES

- Don't be shy to ask.

- Love your family, they'll always be there for you.

- Be the person your family and friends can rely on.

- Sometimes you have to break the rules.

## CHAPTER 13

# THEY REACH THE SKY

*'Everything will be okay. Maybe not today,*
*maybe not this week, but it will be okay.*
*I promise you.'*

I THOUGHT I'D finish with this story because a) it was the most recent big event of my life by the time I finished writing and b) it just about sums up everything I've been talking about in the previous 12 chapters. I swear to you that what I'm about to tell you is all true. Buckle up. It's a mad story.

Allow me to set the scene. It's May 2023 and life is pretty good. The twins are on the way. We had a gender reveal party and everyone now knows we're having daughters. I'm made up. The pregnancy has gone smoothly and Sinéad is 33 weeks. Meanwhile, I'm getting loads of interesting offers of work doing some of the things I love. In March, I was asked to do some presenting work for ITV at the Cheltenham Festival and I'm getting regular work with talkSPORT. I love my sport so this is all a dream for me.

And then one day the phone rings and I get an offer I can't believe.

'Can you manage West Ham, Tom?'

Is the Pope Catholic? Of course, I can!

Now before we all get excited, I need to explain. It wasn't a call up to save the first team from the relegation scrap they were in at the time. This was to manage a team of West Ham legends in a tournament being staged in the USA. The televised competition was called the TST, which stands for The Soccer Tournament (we'll forgive the Americans for calling it soccer instead of football). It took place for the first time in 2023 at WakeMed Soccer Park in Cary, North Carolina and billed itself as the 'defining world champion-ship for 7v7 soccer'. The format followed the World Cup structure, with 32 teams playing in groups and knockout stages over four days.

The West Ham squad comprised heroes and legends. There was Carlton Cole, Marlon Harewood, Anton Ferdinand, Hayden Mullins, Jack Collison, Ricardo Vaz Tê, Luis Boa Morte, Jimmy Walker, Matt Jarvis, Elliot Ward, David Martin, Kyel Reid, Tyrone Mears, Frank Nouble and Zavon Hines. All players I'd spent the last decade watching and cheering for. The squad also included academy gradu-ates Archie Woods and Keenan Forson and Harry Potter actor and West Ham fan Hero Fiennes Tiffin.

The winning team would get prize money of $1 million to share between them and the whole thing was being filmed by a Netflix crew for a documentary. It was the best oppor-tunity I'd ever been offered.

I'll be honest, I didn't have to think too hard about saying yes except for one thing. Sinéad was pregnant with our twins.

But she still had a month to go and everything had been fine up to that point. She was healthy, the babies were healthy. We had a chat and she was pleased for me and knew how much it meant. And it wasn't like I was going away for weeks or going somewhere remote. It was America. There were hundreds of flights to the UK every day. Her sisters came to stay at the house with her and Henry while I was away.

The night before I flew out David, one of the key managers at the club, came to my house and dropped off my kit. I was on cloud nine. It was like a dream. I was so proud. It was like I'd been preparing my whole life for this opportunity.

The following morning Anton Ferdinand (Rio's more talented brother) turned up at my house to go to the airport with me. Colin the Cabbie (another Hammers fan) came to take us to Heathrow and on the way we picked up Elliot Ward. I sat in the back with my new mates, both legends, having a joke and talking about the team. I had to pinch myself. It took my mind off the fact that I hate flying.

At the airport all the other players started turning up. It was getting better and better. The flight was called and we all boarded. As usual I began to get nervous. The team was scattered all over in economy and when I found my seat I was on my own, sitting in a row of three with an American couple. I said hello and mentioned that I was a nervous flyer.

'Don't you worry,' the lady said. 'We'll take care of you.'

I found out they were called David and Dana. They lived in North Carolina, and they turned out to be the best flight buddies. I chewed their ears for the whole flight, telling them about my life, the twins and some of the mad things that were happening to me. They were great company. Without them, it would have been a miserable eight hours. We had a few beers together. They talked about their life in America, I talked about London and fish and chips.

As we came in to land at Raleigh airport David said, 'Tom, do you mind if I say a prayer for you?'

It was a lovely gesture. No one had ever done that for me before. He wished me all the best and good luck with the twins. We landed without a hitch, and we swapped numbers and promised to keep in touch.

I disembarked from the plane and was one of the last off because I was at the back of the plane. The rest of the team had already got through immigration by the time I was called forward.

I stood in front of the passport officer, said hello and handed him my passport. He looked at me, put my passport in a Ziplock bag and said, 'Sir, I need you to come with us.'

Seemingly out of nowhere two massive security guards appeared, stood either side of me and took me into a holding room where they told me to sit down at a table.

'Mate, what's going on?' I said. I don't mind admitting, I was shitting myself. These geezers were not messing around and they would not tell me anything.

After a couple of minutes two armed police officers came into the room. One of them took the bag with my passport, removed it and looked at it, then looked at me. They both sat opposite me and one of them spoke.

'What are your intentions for coming to the USA?' he said.

'I'm the manager of West Ham,' I said. 'I'm here to win a football tournament … I mean soccer.'

He looked at the passport again.

'Mr Skinner,' he said. 'You've been red flagged. You filled out your ESTA did you not?'

An ESTA is a form you fill out to get your visa.

'I did,' I replied.

'Thanks to newspaper reports we know you have a conviction for handling stolen goods and you didn't notify us of this when you filled in your ESTA,' he said.

I thought back to the form.

'Honestly, there was nowhere on the form to say if you have a criminal conviction or not,' I explained, 'plus I'm dyslexic so I'm not good with forms anyway.'

I couldn't believe I'd got that far and was faced with an early bath.

I started sweet-talking the cops.

'Come on mate, that was years ago. It's ancient history. I'm a respectable public figure now and I'm part of a big tournament that's bringing great publicity to North Carolina. I'm managing the mighty West Ham.'

'What's a West Ham?' the other cop asked.

I laughed and so did they.

'Okay,' the main cop said finally. 'As you are with West

Ham and it's an event that the whole state is behind, on this one occasion we'll let you in. Just make sure you fill in the form properly next time. Have a great time.'

Result!

By the time I managed to get out of the airport the players had got on the team coach and left without me so I had to get a cab to the hotel where I checked in and caught up with everyone and then went to bed as it was late by then.

The following day, 31 May, was a full day of preparation for the tournament that began on 1 June. It was a brilliant day. We did some training, and I taught a lot of Americans to say bosh. We had a laugh and bonded. I got into the managerial role and we discussed tactics, which, in a nutshell were get out there, give it 110 per cent and win. We went out for a lovely Italian meal and back at the hotel I told the squad that we needed an early night and to meet at 8.30 a.m. the following morning to get the coach to the stadium.

Back in my room, I texted Sinéad in the UK where it was five hours ahead. She was going to bed and we both said goodnight. Now, I don't know what it was but I just had a feeling that something wasn't right, but I couldn't put my finger on it. I didn't sleep a wink and at 2 a.m. I stopped trying, got up and went for a walk around the town just to try and clear the anxiety I was feeling. Back in the UK it was 7 a.m. and Sinéad was up so I FaceTimed her and spoke to Henry too.

'What are you up to today?' I asked her. She explained

that she had a routine appointment at the hospital which her sister was going to with her.

'We might get the official due date today,' she said, which was probably going to be around the end of June or early July.

'Brilliant,' I said, 'ring me when you're there so I know how you're getting on.'

I told her I couldn't sleep and she said it was probably just jetlag and that everything was fine back at home.

Nevertheless, back in the room I still couldn't sleep and got up at 6 a.m. and bumped into Zavon Hines. We went to the gym and had a workout and I went for another walk and had breakfast with the players. I started to get into the flow and slowly put any feelings of unease behind me.

After breakfast I went back to my room to get ready, and at 8.20 a.m. I quickly called Sinéad because I knew she was having an appointment at the hospital. She answered the phone on the second ring and all I could hear was her hyperventilating. She couldn't breathe.

'Sinéad ... what's wrong?' I was panicking. She was crying hysterically.

'Try and calm down and talk to me babe,' I urged her. 'What's the matter?'

She managed to compose herself.

'It's not good news Tom,' she said. 'Talk to the doctor.'

She handed the phone to the doctor who explained that the scan showed that one of the twins hadn't grown since the last scan and both their heart rates were low.

'We need to get them out in the next 24 hours. If we don't we could lose the twins and we could lose your wife.'

I felt winded. It was a hammer blow.

'So what's going to happen?' I was trying to think straight, to plan my next move.

'We need to take her into surgery as soon as we can,' the doctor said.

'Okay, can you put her back on the phone please.'

Sinéad was crying still.

'Where are you Tom? I need you here.'

'Listen,' I said, 'everything's going to be fine. You will be fine, the twins will be fine. I need you to take a deep breath and be calm. I will get back there, I promise you.'

'But you're in North Carolina,' she said.

'I've never let you down Sinéad and I'm not about to. I'll be there.'

I finished the call and switched into what I can only describe as manager mode. I called and texted everyone I knew who could help and support Sinéad until I could get back. I called my dad and mum. It was like organising a military operation.

I left the room to get to the coach with my head buzzing and got into the lift and burst into tears. All I could think was that I was 5,000 miles away and I might never see my wife again, my twins might die and all that would be left was me and little Henry and I wasn't there for him.

I walked over to the waiting team, red eyed, with tear-stained cheeks and told them what had happened and that I had to go home. They were all brilliant. I had a plan. The stadium was on the way to the airport so I planned to go there with the team and then get a cab from the stadium to the airport where I'd get the next flight to the UK.

The coach was actually a school bus and on the way I was texting Sinéad and arranging for someone to look after Henry if she was suddenly unable to. My heart hadn't stopped racing.

We arrived at the stadium, I said goodbye to the team and went to find a cab. After running around for 20 minutes it became apparent there wasn't one. *What the fuck am I going to do?*, I thought to myself. And then I saw our coach parked in the car park. I ran over to it and the driver was sitting in his seat having a sandwich and flicking through his phone.

'I need a lift to the airport,' I said, and explained my situation.

He put down his sandwich.

'Hey man, it's family,' he said. 'I'll get that done for you.'

We got to the airport and the driver said he'd wait outside in case I couldn't get a flight. I went in and politely let myself into the front of the queue on the airport ticket sales desk.

'I need the next flight to London, my wife is in serious trouble, please, please can you help me,' I implored.

The lady behind the desk looked at the system.

'I'm so sorry sir, all flights to London are fully booked today, the next available seats are tomorrow,' she said.

'What about another airport, can I get to another airport where there is a flight available? I need to get back to London in the next 24 hours.'

She did some more checking.

'There's a flight that leaves here in four and a half hours to Philadelphia where there's a connection to London 45 minutes after you arrive,' she said. 'That's the only way you'll get a flight to the UK today.'

'I'll take it,' I said.

I looked at my watch, did some calculations and called Sinéad. She told me she was booked in for an emergency c-section at 8 a.m. the following day. I told her I was getting on a flight and I'd be back at 6 a.m. London time.

'I'll be there,' I promised her.

She felt better knowing that I was coming back and scheduled to be there when she went in. I felt better knowing that there was a plan in place. Sinéad had her sisters with her and was calm. Henry was with my mum. I was going to be there when she went in for the c-section. Everything was sweet, or as sweet as it could be. I allowed myself to take a breath and walked outside the airport. I stood there thinking for a minute. I had four hours to kill. There was only one thing to do.

I went back out to the coach.

'Take me to the stadium,' I told the driver. 'I'm going to manage West Ham!'

We raced to the stadium. Kick off was 10.30 a.m. I looked at my watch as I raced through the concourse. It was 10.28 a.m. I sprinted through the crowds, vaulted the barrier and ran onto the pitch as the team were forming a circle for their motivational speech.

I jumped in the middle.

'You're here Tom!' they said.

I explained that everything was gravy and launched into the speech of all speeches.

'We're doing this for my wife. We're doing this for my twins.'

They were cheering. I was crying. It was full of emotion. They took their places on the pitch. I went to the sidelines to dry my eyes and do my job as a coach. The whistle blew. They were beaten 4–2. Same old West Ham.

I didn't care to be honest. The game ended and I said my goodbyes then raced back to the hotel to get my suitcase and on to the airport. At that stage everything was going to plan but as I got to security Sinéad's sister, Siobhan, face-timed me. She was crying her eyes out.

'What is it? What's wrong? I pleaded.

'The babies are coming now,' she said.

'What! What's going on? Put Sinéad on. I need to speak to her.'

Sinéad couldn't speak, she'd been given a sedative.

Between blubs Siobhan explained that Sinéad was surrounded by doctors and being rushed into surgery.

'She's going to die, we're going to lose her,' she sobbed. As I was listening to this, with my heart in my mouth, I was being shuffled forward through security and onto the plane.

I tried to snap Siobhan out of it.

'Stop this Siobhan,' I told her. 'You can't be doing this. You need to be strong for her. Pull yourself together. Don't let her see you like this.'

I wouldn't have it. Nothing was going to happen to my Sinéad.

'Go in there and hold her hand,' I told her.

I boarded the plane and as we started to take off I got a text from Siobhan.

*OMG, the twins have come. You are a dad of twin girls Thomas.* It was signed off with a heart. There was no mention of Sinéad.

I texted back.

*Is my wife okay? Let me know asap.*

As the text went, I lost the signal.

For the next hour and 15 minutes all I could think was that Sinéad was dead. *Why would Siobhan not have mentioned Sinéad? That must mean something is wrong. I'm a widower with a young son and two premature twin daughters.* The flight was torture. It was just me on my own, 35,000 ft in the air in a metal tube with my thoughts that were twisting around in my head. My stomach was in knots.

My anxiety was broken by an announcement over the intercom.

'Cabin crew, ten minutes to landing.'

At least there was some relief in knowing that I would soon be able to make contact with the UK again. But I dreaded what I would find out.

The plane got lower. I could see the trees and buildings. The captain lined up for the runway. We were coming in when, at what must have been less than 100 ft from the runway, the intercom blared.

'Brace! Brace!'

The plane accelerated like I've never felt in my life and climbed suddenly almost vertically. People screamed. I stood up in a panic and fell over. A steward called to me.

'Sir! Get in your seat and get in the brace position.'

The plane shot into the air. All the lockers opened. Objects were flying through the cabin. People cried. Many started praying. Outside there was a loud banging noise coming from the flaps.

Just as suddenly the plane levelled off and slowed down to a normal speed. The captain came on the intercom again.

'Ladies and gentlemen, I'd like to apologise for that. We had to take evasive action and abort the landing because another aircraft had accidentally taxied onto the runway. I have been a Delta Airline pilot for 41 years and that has never happened before. Luckily, we are trained for that.'

Once the adrenaline wore off I realised that we would now land later. I only had a 45-minute turnaround anyway and I still didn't know if my wife was alive.

We circled the airport and landed safely. Everyone clapped and my phone buzzed twice with the most welcome message I've ever received. It was from Siobhan.

*Sinéad is okay. She's in recovery.*

Attached to it was a photo of two beautiful little baby twins with pipes hanging out their mouths and noses because they were so small and needed help breathing and eating. They were 3 lb each.

I messaged back and explained where I was and that I'd nearly crashed but was due to get a connection and would be back soon.

I sprinted off the plane to the gate only to be told that the flight was delayed for an hour. While I was there I told them the story and asked for a cheeky upgrade. They put me in first class and when we finally took off I allowed myself a few drinks to calm my nerves and paid the $35 for the crappy Wi-Fi so I could text Sinéad, who was coming round by then. She said she was feeling groggy and couldn't feel her legs from the anaesthetic, but was okay.

I messaged Col the Cabbie and asked him to collect me from Heathrow. He was waiting for me outside. I got in the cab and burst into tears. All the emotions of the last 24 hours caught up with me and I was overwhelmed.

I got to the hospital and went straight to see Sinéad. We hugged and I sat there with her for a bit before I went to see the twins, who we named Darla and Roma. They looked so helpless, connected to machines in incubators. It was all an emotional blur. I hadn't slept for two days and I was shattered. I said goodbye to Sinéad and went home to see Henry who gave me a big hug and told me he missed me. I picked him up and gave him a cuddle and eventually laid down on the sofa, finally able to relax, knowing everyone I loved was okay and safe.

Siobhan was in the house and she came into the lounge.

'I feel so guilty,' I said to her, 'I was only in the hospital for ten minutes.'

She frowned.

'Tom, it's six in the evening. You've been in the hospital all day.'

I was delirious with exhaustion and didn't know what time of day it was. I couldn't keep my eyes open any longer.

Some people will go through life and try and control everything with plans and strategies and when they hit an unexpected problem they come apart like a Digestive in a mug of tea. It wasn't until I'd got my head around what had happened that I realised that being someone who doesn't tend to plan things was a real advantage, because I'm used to thinking on my feet and finding a way round things, no matter what.

Ultimately, whatever happens in life, you are the only one who can control how you react and what you do. Family is everything, put them first and do what you can to protect them and look after them.

# SKINNER'S SCRIPTURES

- You never know where an opportunity will take you.

- If you don't ask, you don't get.

- Keep a cool head in a crisis.

- There's always a way, you just have to find it.

## EPILOGUE

# BOSHONOMICS

SO NOW YOU know a bit more about me and my life, and hopefully I've given you a few pointers that might help you when you hit tough times, because unfortunately you will. We all do. All you have to remember is that no one's life is perfect, we all have ups and downs. Make the most of the ups and push on through the downs. Be strong, keep marching forward. They don't last. Life can turn around on the flip of a coin and we're all always growing and changing. When I started writing this book I was a father of one with a few mattresses in my van and a few Twitter fans. In the time it took me to finish I've been on panels on LBC Radio with politicians, I've discussed celebrating being English on *Good Morning Britain*, I've spoken at the Oxford Union, I've managed West Ham and I've had twins. That's how much life can change.

I hope you've enjoyed reading this as much as I enjoyed writing it and I wanted to finish with a few more thoughts and some advice.

Bear with me on this, but I reckon that I might be able to do a better job running the country than some of the helmets who have been in charge in the past. I'm not political at all and I don't have a horse in the race, but in my opinion a lot of politics is just common sense. I've done a few interviews where I've been asked my views on certain subjects and I've just given my straight opinion, with no filter. I was genuinely surprised by the amount of people who commented and said I'd make a good prime minister. I don't know about that. I'm not sure the country is ready for the Bosh Party ... but if it was, this would be our manifesto:

## TREASURY

Every single person in the UK should be able to afford a pint of beer or a glass of wine. If you are a working man you should be able to afford a drink at the end of the week. A pint should be a basic human right. It's been in our history for hundreds of years. There should be a free pint for every working person on a Friday after work.

It's time for a fairer tax system. Stop letting the little man take the strain while the big corporations get away with paying less tax than they morally should. With more tax receipts and everyone paying their fair share, we can pay health workers more and attract more doctors and nurses. Did you know doctors study for about ten years and leave medical school with tens of thousands of pounds of debt? A junior doctor starts out at just shy of £30,000 a year. That doesn't go far nowadays. Even in private care a surgical procedure costs between £30,000 and £40,000. The surgeon only gets around £600 of that. No wonder we have a shortage of healthcare workers.

## HEALTH

Free fruit and veg seeds for all would mean everyone would have a ready supply of healthy food in their gardens or in disused community spaces. Kids wouldn't have to stuff their faces full of chocolate or go to school with a breakfast of an energy drink and a Twix because they can open their door and pick a pear or an apple. No wonder 60 per cent of the population is overweight or obese. Healthy food isn't accessible. If it's there on your doorstep, you'll eat it.

# ENVIRONMENT

The UK farming sector is fucked. We get 90 per cent of our food from abroad. The UK is one of the few countries that doesn't have a fair trade farming system. Farmers get tucked up. The supermarkets batter them down on price until they can't produce the food for what it costs. There are market traders who go and buy their stock from Aldi because it's cheaper than buying from a UK wholesale market. They wait until the stores open and clear the shelves, then sell it on their stalls. How can independent UK retailers compete with that? Unfortunately, we've all got used to buying fruit and veg too cheap. You can buy broccoli for 27 pence. It's actually devalued good nutritious food. Back in the day we used to grow most of what we ate in the UK. Random things like pineapples or avocados were luxuries. We need more fruit trees. Everyone used to have a fruit tree in their garden. We have a cherry tree in our garden, they are lovely. Now everyone has astroturf and no plants. When you go to Spain, they have orange and lemon trees in their streets and everyone can help themselves. Why don't we do that here? We grow the best apples in the world here.

## LAW AND ORDER

The justice system in the UK is in a right state. That's because no one has any respect for the police. It starts from the ground up. The cops used to be hard bastards, now it's just a job at the end of the day for a lot of them and if you look at them a lot of them are overweight. They need to get themselves down to Bosh Gyms where Hughie will sort them out and toughen them up.

## INDUSTRY

We have a productivity problem in this country and that's because people don't have a proper breakfast. You cannot crack on and smash the day unless you've had a good bit of breakfast. That's why I have dinner for breakfast. Wake up and have a proper meal, then you're full and ready to go. The day is yours; your belly is full and you have energy to burn. There should be free alarm clocks for everyone, but they should all be set for 5 a.m. That way you can get up and make your money early.

We need to support small businesses because small businesses are the backbone of the economy. All small businesses generate taxes and that funds the NHS. They are dropping like flies at the moment, they are struggling and so there is less money going into the NHS. If we lose small businesses we lose the NHS. Fact.

## TRANSPORT

The trains are far too expensive. It's cheaper to get a black cab from London to Birmingham than it is to get a train. How do you work that out? It's cheaper to fly to Scotland than it is to get a train. Public transport should be affordable. You want to save the environment and get more cars off the road? Then invest in the trains better. Stop the strikes because they get paid well as it is. There are plenty of people who would like to earn what rail workers earn. My mate works on the railways, he works three hours a night and earns £250. That's a decent hourly rate.

## FOREIGN AFFAIRS

It's time to take Xi Jinping and Vladimir Putin down to Dino's for a summit. I'll sit them down and have a frank chat with them.

'Listen you helmets, what the fuck do you think you're doing? Calm down.'

They need a mug of tea and a sunshine curry.

## SKINNER FOR PM?

Bosh!

# ACKNOWLEDGEMENTS

A BIG THANK you to Mum and Dad for giving me the best start in life. Legends. Nobody works harder than them. That is where my get up and go comes from.

My family and friends – Uncle Steve, Big Lanks, Collins, Cole, Rylan, Kimberley, Warren, Ben Wilson, Sam McCarthy, Tony Turner, Al Bud, Big Hughie, Ben The Albanian, Robert Hisee (the UK's Number 1!), Dan Williams, Charles, Bill Ford and Big Mark RIP. Without them none of the stories in this book would exist.

Ernie and Terry at Dino's Cafe (the best cafe in the world) for cooking me the 'boshest' breakfasts.

The 'Guvnor of words' Nick Harding for helping me bring these stories to life.

Kelly Ellis and her team at HarperCollins for allowing me to publish my own book. I'm just a geezer from Romford who loves grafting.

My Press Bosh team at Press Box PR for their help and guidance.